ENJOYING THE PRESENCE
OF GOD

ENJOYING
THE PRESENCE
OF GOD

Studies in the Psalms

D. Martyn Lloyd-Jones
Edited by Christopher Catherwood

CROSSWAY BOOKS
Eastbourne

Cover photo: W. Geiersperger, Cephas picture library

ISBN 1 85684 023 9

Production and Printing in England for
C R O S S W A Y   B O O K S
Glyndley Manor, Pevensey, Eastbourne, East Sussex BN24 5BS by
Nuprint Ltd, Station Road, Harpenden, Herts AL5 4SE.

CONTENTS

1 *THE FOLLY OF UNBELIEF*

The fool hath said in his heart,
'There is no God.'
(PS 14:1).

THERE CAN BE NO DOUBT at all but that the greatest matter confronting every man and woman born into this world is that which is put before us by this statement in Psalm 14. Nothing, surely, can be more important than this question of our relationship to God.

There are, indeed, many great questions confronting us and confronting the world in which we live, matters which are not only occupying the minds of statesmen but also of common people. If we think at all seriously about our existence in the world, it is very right that we should be talking about and considering all these national and international problems that arise. Mankind, with its scientific and technological discoveries, has succeeded in doing so many things which have tremendous and terrible possibilities for the future. And yet, I repeat, this question that is put before us here by the psalmist transcends all those other questions in importance. So that is why I shall not be dealing with such things as nuclear warfare or national and international politics nor with any one of these matters, because, as I understand my calling, my privilege is to consider with you something which is infinitely more important than all those things, even put all together.

Why is that? For this good reason: we are dealing here with something which is absolutely certain, and which goes on and continues, whatever may happen with respect to any one of the other questions. Whether there is war or not, my relationship to God still remains. Even though there be no war, I know that my life in this world is limited and that I still have to face this question. And indeed, should war come and should we find hell let loose again upon the face of the earth, then I think it is clear that there will be nothing more important at that moment than our relationship to God. If our cities are reduced to a mass of rubble, then our interest will not be in their buildings or their universities or anything like that. No, we shall be face to face with our own destiny, and that brings us at once to this question of our relationship to God. So this is incomparably the greatest and the most important matter that can ever face men and women while they are in this world.

Now there are many attitudes towards this question, but at this point I only want to consider with you this particular one which is here described by the psalmist. It is the attitude which says, 'There is no God.' This, as you know, is a very common attitude. There are many who take up this position, who say that and who plan their lives and order their existence on this supposition. They say, 'I don't believe in God, and'—they add—'the fact that there is no God makes no difference to my life at all.'

So let us consider what the psalmist has to say about that attitude. You will notice that he makes a very blunt assertion. What he says about all people who are in that position is simply that they are fools—'The *fool* hath said in his heart, There is no God.' Now, we must emphasise here that the psalmist is making a universal statement. He does not say, 'Some of the people who say that there is no God are fools'; he says, 'Every one of them is.' He does not say, 'Of course, there are fools who say this sort of thing, but on the other hand there are great and learned and educated people who also say it.' Not at all! He makes a universal statement without any qualification or exceptions whatsoever. Or, to put it the other way round, he says, 'Anyone who says, "There is no God," is just a fool.'

What is a fool? Well, the real meaning of the word is that he is a superficial person. The fool is a man who does not think. He is always contrasted with the wise man or, as the psalmist puts it, with the man of understanding. He says in verse 2, 'The Lord looked down from heaven upon the children of men, to see if there were any that did understand.' So the fool you see, is a man who lacks understanding; he lacks the ability to think clearly; he is a man who acts in an impetuous manner, who does not consider the consequences—that is the biblical meaning of the word 'fool'. He is someone who acts in an idiotic manner, he is lacking in reason and insight.

'Dear me,' says someone, 'surely is this a most extraordinary statement. Is that true today? Is that your contention? Are you asserting that what the psalmist said in his generation is still the simple truth today?' Well, I am concerned to establish this very proposition. I am a preacher because I believe in the depth of my being that people who say that there is no God are just fools! And the business of preaching is to enlighten them, to show them their error; it is to expose them to the utter folly of the position that they have taken up. I do so in love. I do so because of my concern for any such person who may be reading these words. There is nothing to me so tragic as that people should be fools and that in their folly they should say, 'There is no God.'

So then, how do I establish this? How could the psalmist have established it in his day? Well, I want to reason the thing out with you. I say the times are so serious that I need not remind you that I am doing this not because I delight in argumentation or disputation, nor because I like conducting this kind of enquiry in an intellectual and in a theoretical manner. I hope to show you before I have finished that, as we have already seen, this is the vital matter of all matters, the things that depend upon it are so momentous and so terrifying that I feel it is my duty to put this matter as simply and as plainly and as directly as I can to anybody who is prepared to listen.

Here, then, is the contention: that men and women who say in their hearts that there is no God are fools; and the first respect in which this is true of them is that they are people who listen overmuch to their hearts—'The fool hath said in his *heart*, There is no God.' They are, according to the psalmist, governed by their desire; their outlook is determined by this which he calls the 'heart', which is the seat of the sensibilities. They are governed by what they like and by what they want to do, rather than by certain other things. It is a decision they have arrived at, says the psalmist, in their hearts.

So why is this a foolish thing to do? Well, let me put it in the form of a number of contrasts. Here are people who are fools because they listen to their hearts and their desire, instead of listening to that sense which is within them, as it is in every man and woman born into this world, a sense of God. Now people, of course, may try to stifle that; they may try to argue it down; they may try to brow-beat it, but what I am asserting is that in every human being there is a sense of God. And, of course, this is rarely granted because many today who do not believe in God think they can explain away this sense of Him, though they may admit that it is there. But the fact is that there is in all of us a feeling that at the back of everything there is this eternal being and that behind everything that is seen is the great, unseen, eternal God. There is this natural sense of reverence in us all—perhaps accompanied by an element of fear—but it is there.

You can study anthropology, as has been done, and you can go and investigate the condition of the most primitive peoples that are in the world at this moment. You will find them in many places and you will find that among them all there is, nevertheless, this sense of God. Many of them worship stones and trees, and find spirits in animals and so on, but they have all got this sense of a supreme being, of a God who is at the back of and beyond all the other gods that they worship. Now I say that those who brush that aside and who listen and who are governed by what they want to be the truth and what they would like to be the truth, in order that they may live a certain kind of life, are just being fools. Surely it is our business to pay very close and careful attention to anything that is elemental within us; to anything that is profound within us. Men and women who dismiss something that seems to be an innate part of their personality and of their very being are, I suggest, fools! And those who say, 'There is no God', are guilty of doing that. They are going against a voice within themselves that says there is a God.

But that is only the first point. In the same way, such people go against the voice of their conscience. For again this is something that is beyond dispute. We all have a conscience within us. We often wish we had not, but we do have it, and when we do something that is wrong, our conscience tells us so and it condemns us. It makes us feel miserable. We may pass through an agony of remorse, if not of repentance, and that is the voice of conscience speaking; the voice that says, 'You shouldn't have done it! That's wrong! That isn't true! That's against this God, a sense of whom you have within you.' There it is in the whole of mankind, a conscience which we cannot explain. And yet, you see, here is a man, says the psalmist, who violates that in the same way. He does not listen to it; he does not pay attention to it; he is not governed by it.

So what is he governed by? Ah, he is governed by another type of life that he has conjured up; he sees other people living it and he says to himself, 'What a wonderful thing it would be if I could go and live that sort of life!' But he is a bit afraid of that, because it is not godly and his conscience condemns him, but he says, 'Very well then, there is no God. Perhaps, after all, I've been fooling myself.' So, in order to live that life, and because he cannot do the two things at the same time, he has to say, 'There is no God.' But in doing that he is violating the voice of his conscience, as he has already violated this sense of God that is within him.

But, and this is the point I particularly want to emphasise, such people are fools because they do not use and do not listen to their understanding. That is, as we have seen, the psalmist's contention: 'The Lord looked down from heaven upon the children of men, to see if there were any that did *understand*.... Have all the workers of iniquity no knowledge,' He asks, 'who eat up my people as they eat bread?' Here is the final charge against these men and women and it is, of course, at this point that we see most clearly and plainly the fact that they are fools.

Now, I want first to look at this point in general because there are two main objections which are brought very volubly against it. The average person today, hearing a statement like that would respond by saying, 'My dear Sir, do you know that you're preaching in 1957 and not in AD 57 or something like that? To say that people today have no understanding because they don't believe in God! Why, it's *because* of their understanding that they don't believe in God!'

That is the argument is it not? It is said that these people do not believe in God because of their knowledge; because of their great brains and their wonderful ability. Furthermore, the argument goes, the only people who still believe in God are these primitive types who have not yet developed; or these psychological cases, these psychopaths or people who deliberately put their heads in the sand and will not look at the evidence and will not face the facts.

So let me meet that argument. The psalmist's contention is that these people are fools! And they are fools because they do not act on their understanding but on their desires. How do I establish this? Well, let me ask a question: is this disbelief in God confined to the learned and to the people of knowledge? You see, if this argument is right, then all the ignorant people in the world would be believers in God; but the learned people—the people of knowledge and especially scientific knowledge—every one of them would not believe in God. But is that so? We know perfectly well that for every learned, intelligent person you can show me in the world today who does not believe in God, I can show you one who is unlearned and ignorant and lacking in intelligence and ability. Oh, it is a wonderful thing to hear these picked intellects speaking on the media; they do not believe in God, but I can find you five or six people on the street or wherever you like, who say exactly the same thing as they do.

So is this denial of God based upon learning? Why do ignorant, unintelligent people say exactly the same thing? And it is an interesting and a rather important point at the present time,[1] religion—belief in God and the worship of God—is more popular among the intelligent people in this country than it is among the others. Indeed, this is a charge that is very often hurled at the church, because of the statistics. 'Ah,' people say, 'the Christian church, is just middle class; it doesn't touch the masses of the people.' Now, that is a very important statement, is it not? I am not saying anything against any particular group in society, but I must indicate this: that religion is most successful today in the universities, among the people who are in such places of learning because they have brains and intelligence. It is succeeding there much more than in suburbia, much more than it is among the masses of the people. The fact is that the masses of the people today are unconcerned, and the Christian church somehow or another is not touching them. So, all I would comment therefore, is that it is not primarily a matter of intelligence. The facts prove that it is not.

But let me put that in a still stronger form. Not only can I thus establish that the unintelligent and illiterate and people who have no culture do not believe in God, I can on the other side show you how men of knowledge, of learning, of culture and of science have been some of the greatest believers in God and in Christ that the church and the world has ever known. For instance, people only know about Isaac Newton in terms of his scientific discoveries and theorisings and his brilliant hypotheses, they know about him and the apple falling and so on. They do not know that Isaac Newton spent most of his time in studying the Scriptures and in writing books about prophecy, and he himself regarded his religious work as being altogether more important than his other work. Yet he was one of the great towering geniuses of all time in the scientific realm. Blaise Pascal, the brilliant mathematician, lived in the same century and he, too, believed in God. I could go on, but, you see, the moment you begin to analyse this argument that the modern disbelief in God is the result of knowledge and learning and understanding, then it just does not hold water for a second.

No, it is clear that whatever the explanation may be of the failure of men and women to believe in God, it is not the explanation of knowledge and of learning. It is because these people are fools and are governed by something else rather than by their understandings.

But let me say a word about the second objection, which is this: I can imagine someone saying, 'Well, of course, all that you have just been saying might have been quite all right a hundred or perhaps two hundred years ago, but that is not really the position now. The majority today are not interested in God and in Christ and in the church and in salvation because of our recent knowledge. Darwin, you see, wrote his book in 1859, and the spread of biological knowledge, our knowledge of psychology, the study of comparative religion and all these other things—that is what has done it. Anyone who is really aware of all this latest knowledge is driven to saying that "There is no God".'

But the simple answer to that argument is that in the time that David wrote this psalm, people were saying exactly the same thing. There is nothing new about not believing in God, it is the oldest thing in the world to deny Him. This is what I find so pathetic, that people think it is clever not to believe in God; that it is modern; that it is something new; that it is something wonderful! But here is a man, King David, writing all this a thousand years before Christ—nearly three thousand years ago, and there were people saying then, 'There is no God;' just what the clever people are saying today, who try to argue that they are saying it in terms of some latest esoteric knowledge that they have been let in to and which other people still do not have. But is it not clear that this has nothing at all to do with knowledge as such?

No, it is a question of understanding, and that is a very different thing. Men and women may be very able with a lot of book knowledge, but it does not mean that they have understanding nor that they have wisdom. They can be aware of numbers of facts, but they may be fools in their own personal lives. Have we not known such people? I have known men in some of the learned professions, I would take their opinion without a moment's hesitation because of their knowledge and because of their learning. But sometimes I have known some of those men to be utter fools in their own personal lives. I mean by that that they behaved like lunatics, as if they had not a brain at all. They have behaved in exactly the same way as a man who had never had their educational advantages and who had none of their great knowledge.

They drank too much even as he did, they were guilty of adultery even as he was.

There is all the difference in the world between knowledge and an awareness of facts, and wisdom and real understanding; because though people may have great brains and may know a number of things, they may still be governed by their lusts and passions and desires and that is why they are fools. They want to live the kind of life that the psalmist describes here. 'They are altogether become filthy,' he says. 'There is none that doeth good'; and it is because they want to be filthy that they say, 'There is no God.' So there is my first reason for calling such people fools. They are men and women who listen to their heart, their desires; they are governed by what they want to do rather than by true understanding.

But let me come to a second point. I want to show, in a much more positive way, how these people really fail to exercise this true understanding, and this is something that I can demonstrate to you in two ways.

The first is that they arrive at momentous conclusions on insufficient evidence and, surely, anyone who does that is behaving like a fool. Fools are those who do not reason a thing through, they jump to conclusions; they are governed by their prejudices or, as we have seen, by their passions and lusts and desires. It is the mark of a fool always to draw important deductions from inadequate evidence, and anyone who says that 'there is no God' is guilty of that.

So let me try to prove my point. What are these arguments that such people bring forward? We cannot, clearly, deal with all of them, but let us look at some. Here is a very common one: there are thousands of people in the world today who say, 'I don't believe there is a God,' and when you ask, 'Why not?' they reply, 'Well, it's quite simple. If there is a God, why are there wars?' Or, 'If there is a God, why are there spastic children?' Or again, 'If there is a God, why are there earthquakes and pestilences and things like that?' And on that kind of reasoning, and on that alone, they have come to the conclusion that 'there is no God'.

Now it is amazing how intelligent people can reason and argue like that. I had a conversation once with a highly intelligent professional man who came to me and asked if he might talk to me about these things. He told me that he did not believe in God and when I asked what the reason was for his unbelief, the only reason that he could produce was that his wife had had, for a while, to endure a very painful illness. And that to him was a proof that there was no God.

Well, of course, the argument was a very simple one. I first had to show him that he had arrived at that tremendous conclusion on that one bit of evidence alone. Had he ever thought that perhaps it was a part of the purpose of God to allow this in order to bring something else to pass? I said, 'How have you and your wife normally lived with respect to God? Have you worshipped Him regularly? Have you lived to His praise and glory in the whole of your lives?' He had to admit as an honest man that they had not. They had been living for themselves; they rarely thought of God at all and they certainly never attended a place of worship. They had been living an entirely godless life and yet, because his wife had pain—'there is no God'.

'Now then,' I said, 'It has not occurred to you obviously that perhaps God permitted your wife to have this pain in order to make you both think seriously about God and, perhaps, come to have this conversation with me. God has blessed you, but you have not thanked Him; you have ignored Him altogether. So perhaps God has chastised you now in order to bring you to your senses.' Then I went on, 'I have known many people who, looking back across their lives, have said with the psalmist, "It is good for me that I have been afflicted" because "before I was afflicted I went astray" ' (Ps 119:71&67). 'Do you know anything about that?' I asked. 'Have you not thought about it?' No, he had not thought about it. So I said, 'My dear Sir, if you and I do not understand ourselves and other people and the workings of their minds, how do you think you can so easily understand God and say, "because He does not do this, then there is not a God"? Do you see the conclusion you are drawing on such flimsy evidence?' He had never thought about it at all!

I cannot stay with this argument now, but there are thousands of people who do not believe in God because of the problem of pain, and yet the answer to that problem is a very simple one. The Bible gives it in many places and there are books that expound it; it is so easy to explain and yet these people say, just on that one bit of evidence, 'There is no God'! Simple! QED! No, men and women who reason and argue like that, though they may be very learned and very brilliant, are just behaving like fools.

Then, look at the other evidence, the evidence from the so-called proofs of psychology. People say, 'Psychology has taught us,' or, 'Psychology proves and demonstrates.' Now I could go into this, but we must move on and it is not my business in a sense to do that; but I am making this point in case there may be somebody reading this who up until this moment has said, 'Of course, the only people who believe in God are these ignoramuses who know nothing.' I am simply trying to show you that we who believe in God do know something about these things, and psychology has proved and can prove nothing at all. Psychology is based on pure theory. The popular psychology is, indeed, based upon insanity and the study of insanity. Freud's whole system is based upon such a study, the abnormal which is transferred to the normal, and then the mighty deductions are drawn. So it is no use saying that psychology proves anything. It puts up its theories and its suppositions but you must not call that a proof. To base your position upon that, I say, is to behave in a foolish manner.

And then, of course, there is the great question of evolution. 'Ah,' people say, 'men and women used to think that God had created the world and that He had created man, but we know now that that is not so. We know that everything has come out of primitive slime and that that came from some gases...' and so on and back you go! 'Science has established it and proved it!' Well, I must just say the same thing again. It is simply a scientific statement to say that evolution has not proved anything. Evolution is a theory and nothing but a theory and there are many different theories of evolution, some of which cancel one another right out. Indeed, science proves nothing, because there is not such a thing as 'science', and when you say, 'science proves' what you mean is that certain scientists say this or that, which is a very different thing. But, you see, on this kind of evidence, there are people who say, 'I no longer believe in God.' I say this is folly.

Then we have comparative religion and all these other matters, and in every single case the answer is the same. All these things are but theories, suppositions, ideas conjured up in the minds of men to try to explain the facts. None of them is adequate, all of them are criticised and there are the rival theories and the rival schools. And so I maintain that anyone who draws the momentous conclusion that 'there is no God' on that sort of evidence is a fool.

But look at it the other way round. Such people are doubly guilty. They take their little bits of evidence and on them they draw this important conclusion, but also they do not face the other evidence, the vast, the tremendous evidence on the other side. 'What do you mean?' asks someone. Well, first of all, I really do mean the evidence of creation. I really do mean the world and the cosmos in which we live. I confess I am baffled that anybody should believe that this amazing universe in which we find ourselves is but the result of accident and chance. I must confess I am in many ways thrilled and I am moved as I have been reading about this mysterious thing that has just happened and about which everybody is talking at the present time, this satellite.[2] Have you considered it?

I am not referring now to the cleverness or the ability of man, though it is indeed a tremendous thing that the human mind can take this satellite, as they call it, and shoot it up into that space and that it is there circling the earth. However, I am referring even more to the fact that round our globe there is earth's atmosphere; and then you can get beyond that to this extraordinary 'space', as it were, and then beyond that again there is something else; and this globe is suspended in all that and so are the other bodies— the moon, the sun, the stars and the constellations. Have you thought of it? Have you tried to? 'The mysterious universe' as the late Sir James Jeans called it. And I am asked to believe all this just happened, that there is no mind at the back of all that!

So where has all this come from? And how does it all consist and hold together? How does it all keep going? Is all this ordered universe, this amazing cosmos, the mere accidental, fortuitous result of collisions or of gases suddenly condensing? The thing, I say, is unthinkable! As a man who was privileged to learn a little science and who still has an interest in it, I say my mind cannot accept such a statement.[3] It is madness, it is folly!

And then look at man himself. Are you really satisfied that man is an accident? That he has just come into being, we know not why, nor for what purpose, nor to what end? My dear friend, you are insulting humanity. You are insulting yourself. Man stands up as a protest against it all. There is only one explanation of man and that is God! Man is too big to be explained in such terms. He is more marvellous than the cosmos itself, this little microcosm which we call 'man'.

And then have you ever considered the evidence of history? Go and read it. Read your secular history and read Old Testament history. Can you explain all that apart from God? Can you explain the Jews in particular? Look at them. Why have they persisted? Where have they come from? How do you explain their whole story, in the Old Testament and since? I say there is only one explanation of the Jews and that is God!

Have you ever considered the evidence of prophecy as we find it in the Old Testament? Have you ever considered the fact that there were things foretold eight hundred years and more before they ever happened? Have you ever written down on paper the facts concerning the birth and the life and the death and the resurrection of the Lord Jesus Christ? Have you gone back to the Old Testament and, as He Himself said, have you found them there? Have you found how it was all predicted and prophesied, going back even to Genesis 3:15 and coming right the way through? How do you explain prophecy? There is only one explanation: it is God, who sees the end from the beginning and orders all things after the counsel of His own eternal will and wisdom. It is God, controlling history, biblical history, all history. Have you ever read books on the latest discoveries of archeology? They confirm this biblical history.

But over and above all this evidence I ask you to look at a person called Jesus of Nazareth. He belongs to history, you know. We all recognise that by numbering the years as we do. Yes! He did live! And He died under Pontius Pilate. He is in history—secular history recognises Him. There He is! Look at Him! How do you explain Him? Can you get rid of Him? There is only one way to explain Him and that is God!

And indeed, how do you explain the Christian church herself? Even as she is today, how do you explain her persistence? How did this despised sect become the official religion of the Roman Empire after three centuries? How do you explain the mighty revivals in her history which are also acknowledged in secular history, the Reformation and these other revivals, how do you explain them? Where have they come from? How do you account for them? Can men and women bring these things to pass? Of course they cannot! It is God!

And then, finally, take the great saints of the centuries. You read the account of the greatest benefactors that this world has ever known and you will find that they have been men who believed in God. We are all glad to have hospitals, are we not? We are glad that they are there when we and our loved ones are taken ill and when we need some operation; we are grateful for them and we thank God for them. The oldest hospital in London, St Bartholemew's, was founded by a religious man called Rahere over eight hundred years ago. Hospitals have come from godly people who believed in God, and so have all the other beneficent actions. Men like Lord Shaftesbury and William Wilberforce did what they did because of their belief in God and in Christ.

Do away with a belief in God and you wipe out the greatest saints, the greatest benefactors that the world has ever known. That is some of the evidence that these people ignore and dismiss when they say, 'There is no God.' They draw their conclusions out of the flimsiest evidence and they neglect and ignore this mighty evidence.

But, finally, let me put it like this: my third reason for calling such people fools is because, in that way and for the two reasons that we have just considered, they do not hesitate to risk their whole eternal life and their whole eternal future. 'Ah, but,' they say, 'I don't believe there is anything after death.' Well, you may not believe it, but can you prove it? And I say that in the light of the evidence that I have just been adducing, anyone who is prepared to risk it is a fool! A man who does anything on inadequate security and evidence is a fool. Look at the man who gambles away a fortune. 'Will it stop at my number?' he cries. He risks his whole fortune on it! What do you say afterwards? 'What a fool! Fancy risking everything on just that, on the number on a dice!'

And yet, this is the position here. You cannot prove that there is not a life after death. You do not know what is going to happen to you when you die, and yet you say, 'I'm prepared to risk it!' Are you? What if the Bible is right and that after death men and women who do not believe in God go on to all eternity in misery and wretchedness in an endless, useless remorse, kicking themselves because of their utter folly? Yes, then they will have opened their eyes and they will have seen Christ! And they will have seen God! And they will know that there is a God and they will see that they threw it all away and said, 'There is no God' because of some things they wanted to do for a moment. They 'sold [their] birthright for a mess of pottage' and for less; they jeopardised their whole eternal destiny on that flimsy evidence and on those suppositions and theories. Oh, my dear friend, the thing is so terribly serious. We are in this passing world and it is becoming more uncertain almost every day. What is going to happen next? Man may suddenly do something and the whole universe will be shattered and you and I with it. And what then?

Not to consider that; not to have some grounds for your decision and for your action, is just to proclaim that you are a fool. But this is the heartbreaking thing about it. If God were *only* just and righteous and holy... well, I was almost going to say that in a sense there would be some excuse for a man or woman who does not believe in Him; but there would not be any excuse even then. But the thing that finally makes such people utter fools is when you consider what they refuse; what they reject. They want to live this other kind of life that is so popular with the world; it seems so glamorous and it is going to lead to this, that and the other— marvellous freedom and emancipation—they are going to have their fill. They do not even stop to think that when they are middle aged they will be rather tired of it, and when they are old, lying on a bed somewhere perhaps, with everything gone, like the Prodigal in the far land with no one to attend to them. They have not even considered that, still less have they considered what lies beyond it.

But look at what they have rejected and spurned; look what they have refused! There is no life, even in this world, that is comparable to the godly life. It is a clean life; it is a pure life; it is a holy life, a life lived in fellowship and communion with God and with Christ. It is a life lived among the people who have done the greatest amount of good in this world. I would simply ask you to read; read secular books as well as others, even they prove it and demonstrate it. You see, that other life is so empty. I read recently a statement made by a certain popular novelist who is now an old man facing the end. He has got nothing to look forward to, nothing at all. How terrible! He has always been cynical towards this godly life and there he is now, at the end of his, with nothing. Of course he has not. But this life, even here and now, has joys and pleasures to give us that the world does not know. And as you go on in it, it gets better and better; and as you begin to contemplate the end you are not frightened of death and the grave. You do not say, 'It's the end of everything'; you say, 'I'm going on to spend the whole of my time with Christ in eternity.'

And should all hell be let loose on the earth again, nothing can harm us! Why not? Because our life is that hidden life which is in communion with God and Christ and which is in the safe-keeping of God. We are looking forward to 'an inheritance incorruptible, and undefiled, and that fadeth not away, reserved in heaven' by God, for those who believe in Him (1 Pet 1:4).

So can you not see the folly of saying that 'there is no God'? From every aspect, it is sheer folly. There is no other word for it. It is the absence of understanding; it is the absence of true reasoning and of clear thinking. Be wise, I humbly beseech you, and give proof that you are wise by telling God without delay that though there are still many things you do not understand, you believe that He is and that 'He is a rewarder of them that diligently seek Him' (Heb 11:6). So you are coming to Him to acknowledge your folly; your sin; your shame. You are going to ask Him to have mercy and He will tell you that He has had mercy, that He sent His only Son to die for you and your rebellion and your sin; that He will forgive you freely, take you back to Himself, and give you new life and make you His child and lead you all the way and eventually receive you into glory.

Tell Him! Repent. Acknowledge it; cast yourself upon Him, believe on the Lord Jesus Christ, the Son of God and His wonderful salvation. 'The fear of the Lord is the beginning of wisdom' (Prov 1:7). Prove that you are wise.   Amen.

---

1. This sermon was preached in 1957.
2. 1957 was the year in which the first satellite was launched.
3. Dr Lloyd-Jones trained as a medical doctor.

2   DEAD RELIGION

Psalm 50

I AM ANXIOUS TO CALL your attention to the message of this
entire psalm, because, though it is presented in a number of
different forms and aspects, it really constitutes one essential
argument and message. If, however, you want to have one verse in
your mind more than another, then we may very well select the
twenty-first verse:

> These things hast thou done,
>   and I kept silence;
> Thou thoughtest that I was altogether
>   such an one as thyself:
> But I will reprove thee,
>   and set them in order before thine eyes.

Now, we have considered together the case of the modern
person who says that he or she does not believe in God, that there
is no God. We took our statement from that first statement in
Psalm 14 which says, 'The fool hath said in his heart, there is no
God.' I wonder what you would say if I asked the question: 'Is
there anything that can be more foolish than that?' Is there any
greater folly than the folly of saying that there is no God?

Well, I want to suggest to you that in this fiftieth Psalm there is a suggestion, if not something stronger, that there actually is a greater folly even than that. It is the folly of people who say that they believe in God but who in the tenor of their lives and in the whole of their conduct daily forget God and live exactly as if He did not exist.

Now, surely, this is even greater folly, because whatever else you may say about the people we have been considering, you must at least grant that they are quite consistent with themselves. There is no contradiction in their lives. They say they do not believe in God, and then they go on living on that hypothesis, on that supposition. God is not in all their thoughts, and in no sense does He determine their actions. They do not believe in God and therefore they live without reading the Bible or paying any attention to what it says.

But these other people, surely, are in an even worse state and position because, in addition to their central folly, they are guilty further of being self-contradictory. They proclaim that they believe in God and yet that belief patently and clearly has no influence and no effect upon their lives, their outlook or the whole of their behaviour and living. They are people who contradict what they claim to believe. And that, I suggest to you, is, if anything, even greater folly than the folly of those others who say, 'There is no God,' and then leave it at that.

That is the thing that is set out so clearly and in such a notable manner in this fiftieth Psalm. It is a psalm that is worthy of our careful attention, so let me give you a brief analysis of it.

In the first six verses, God, through the psalmist, calls the people to a judgement, and the judgement, you notice, is announced in a most solemn manner. Here are the terms: 'The mighty God, even the Lord, hath spoken, and called the earth from the rising of the sun unto the going down thereof' (v 1). Not only that: 'He shall call to the heavens from above, and to the earth, that He may judge His people' (v 4). Now, you will always find in the Scriptures that whenever anything of unusual solemnity is being said to the people, heaven and earth are always called to witness. You will find an example of this at the beginning of the prophecy of Isaiah. He contemplates the sin of Israel, and as he delineates it and denounces it, he calls heaven and earth to witness: 'Hear, O heavens and give ear O earth.' 'Is there anything in heaven or earth which is comparable,' he says in effect, 'to the state and the condition and the behaviour of this people?'

So here, in the first six verses, there is this announcement of a most solemn judgement, ending with the statement: 'The heavens shall declare His righteousness: for God is judge Himself.' There is nothing more solemn than that. We are asked, we are invited to pay attention to this momentous announcement of the judgement of God upon mankind particularly here, of course, upon the children of Israel.

Then, in verses 7 to 15, the message of the psalm deals with the whole misunderstanding and misuse of sacrifices and of burnt offerings. It is put in a very graphic way: 'Hear, O my people, and I will speak; O Israel, and I will testify against thee: I am God, even thy God. I will not reprove thee for thy sacrifices or thy burnt offerings, to have been continually before me.' The charge is not that they did not bring them, because they did. No, the charge was, as I shall show you, that they were bringing them in the wrong way. They had misunderstood the whole purpose of the burnt offerings and sacrifices which had been commanded by God. Their entire outlook upon it was wrong and they were misusing them.

And then from verse 16 to verse 22 we see the awful misunderstanding on the part of these people of the law of God and of His covenant with them. 'But unto the wicked God saith, What hast thou to do to declare my statutes, or that thou shouldest take my covenant in thy mouth?' The terrible, appalling misunderstanding, and again the misuse of the law and the covenants of God. Again, it is primarily addressed to the children of Israel, and you find the Apostle Paul doing the same thing in chapters 2 and 3 of his mighty Epistle to the Romans.

Then in the final verse, we have a solemn conclusion and an appeal, a statement of great and vital doctrine: 'Whoso offereth praise glorifieth me: and to him that ordereth his conversation aright will I shew the salvation of God.'

There, then, is a brief analysis of the psalm, but I do not propose to take it with you now in terms of that analysis. I want to put it into its modern setting. For what is put before us here is as true today as it was in the time of the psalmist. We have already seen that there are people today who say that there is no God; yes, but they were also there three thousand years ago, very nearly, in the time of King David when he wrote that psalm. Those people behaved like that then and there are still such people now. And what makes this so solemn is that the people described here in Psalm 50 are not only outside the church, but they are also within the church. These were the children of Israel, and alas, there are many who regard themselves as good church people, members of Christian churches, but who are guilty of this self-same thing today. And that is why it is such a serious matter.

There are many people, as you know, who tell us that though they never go to a place of worship, they are still very interested in religion. They are interested in God, they tell us—'oh yes, tremendously interested'—but they never give any indication of it in their lives. Now, they are the people we are considering but alas, it is even possible to visit the house of God and still be guilty of this very thing.

So in order to show you what I mean, let me put it to you under two main headings. What is the charge that God brings against these people? Well, the first charge is that they do certain things which they should not do; they do certain things wrongly. First of all, instead of taking God's own revelation of Himself, they substitute their own ideas of Him. That runs as a kind of theme throughout the whole psalm; the trouble with these people is ultimately due just to that. We find this in the twenty-first verse, where the psalmist says, 'Thou thoughtest that I was altogether such an one as thyself.' *'Thou thoughtest'*—that is the trouble, and this is the first trouble with this kind of person. They say that they believe in God and that they are interested in Him and in religion. Yes, but the question is: where do they get their ideas from? On what are they basing their views and their whole activity? What is it that they can bring forward as a sanction for their view of God, or their view of religion, or their whole attitude towards the

Christian life? The answer is, of course, that it is determined entirely by themselves.

Now I am sure you will agree that there are many people at the present time who come into this category. We are no longer considering the people who say there is no God at all. We are now dealing with people who say, 'Of course I believe in God; I was brought up to believe in Him, and I have never doubted His existence.' But what are their ideas with respect to God? What are their views as to what He is like, and what is their conception as to what He demands of us? If you talk to such people, you will find that it just comes down to this: that they have made God after their own liking, after their own image. This is how they put it; their speech betrays them immediately; they say, 'What *I* say is this....' And then they proceed to tell you that it is unthinkable that God could do this or that. Some say, 'It's unthinkable that God should ever show what the Bible calls the wrath of God. My whole conception of God excludes the very possibility of wrath. I could not believe in a God who shows this anger against sin and the sinner.' So they cut it out, it is not there. And they do that on the grounds that they cannot believe it, because to them it is unthinkable.

So you see, it is *their* thought that determines everything: 'Thou thoughtest that I was altogether such an one as thyself'—they are making God in their own image, so they do not hesitate to lay down their ideas as to what God is like, and what He ought to do and what He ought not to do. They give their ideas of the love of God, the wrath and the justice of God and of His righteousness— the whole thing is determined by their own thoughts. So they speak about these things but their whole attitude to God and towards religion has no basis and no authority whatsoever apart from their own postulates. That is the first charge that is brought against these people.

The second charge the psalmist brings against them under this heading is that they take only a theoretical interest in God and in religion. Now the words here are very expressive, notice the sixteenth verse: 'But unto the wicked God saith, What hast thou to do to declare my statutes, or that thou shouldest take my covenant in thy mouth?' You see, these people declare, they talk about God's law, they talk about Him and they take His covenant into their mouths. They say that they are very interested in religion; they talk about God, and about morality and ethics; they talk about religion in general and its bearing upon life and what it ought to do and what it ought not to do. But this is the statement about them: *'Seeing thou hatest instruction and casteth my words behind thee.'* What a terrible thing this is!

Here are people whose interest in religion is purely theoretical. It has no influence at all upon their daily life. Having talked so much about God, they live as if He did not exist. They pay lip service to Him but He does not control their lives; He is not the master of their existence. They hate instruction and their lives are not lived in conformity with His commandments—they cast His words behind them. They do not come up to the standard given in the last verse: 'Whoso offereth praise glorifieth me; and to him that ordereth his conversation aright will I shew the salvation of God.'

Now I am not imagining all this. There are many such people in the world, alas, who are interested in religion, who talk about it, and are always ready to have a debate about it. Many of them read books about religion and listen to lectures on the radio about it; perhaps they even listen to sermons in churches about religion and are tremendously interested. But it is purely a detached, intellectual interest, something that they like to play with in their minds and to talk about to others. So the point I am making is this: surely, this is infinitely worse than the position of people who say that there is no God. Indeed, is there anything more terrible than a purely theoretical and academic interest in God and in religion and in the godly life?

But the third and last charge under this particular heading is, as we saw in our analysis at the beginning, that they have a completely false and wrong view of sacrifice and offerings in connection with religion. Now, the psalmist outlines this in detail, so let me summarise the principle. What he is really saying about them is, of course, something that is said repeatedly in the Old Testament about these children of Israel. It is the great burden of the prophets, but some people have misunderstood it and thought that the prophets did not believe in burnt offerings and sacrifices at all. The so-called 'higher critics' constantly tell us that there was a great dispute in the Old Testament between the prophets and the priests. 'The priests,' they say, 'believed in burnt offerings and sacrifices, but the prophets had no use for them at all and told the people not to bother about them.' What a travesty of the Old Testament prophecies!

That was not the problem. The teaching of prophets is not that people should not take their burnt offerings and sacrifices to the temple to God, but that they should take them in the right way. The charge of the prophets is that the children of Israel were misusing and abusing the burnt offerings and the sacrifices; they were taking them in a purely formal and external manner. 'Ah,' they said, in effect, 'the day for taking the burnt offering and the sacrifice has come, so we'll go and take them.' So they took them, but they might as well have stayed at home. They were doing it in a perfectly formal, external, mechanical manner. They were not really troubled as to what it meant, nor as to what it represented. 'Oh, this is one of the things we have to do as a religious people,' they said. Then, having done that, they thought that they had earned merit. 'We are all right again now,' they said, 'we have taken our burnt offerings and sacrifices to the temple and because we have done that we are forgiven and can go on living as we were before.' They believed that it gained merit for them, and that they were, therefore, better people.

But, indeed, it was even worse than that. They did it in such a way and in such a manner as to give the impression that they were conferring a benefit upon God; hence this series of statements which is made here in this devastating section. 'I will take no bullock out of thy house, nor he goats out of thy folds.' Why? 'For every beast of the forest is mine, and the cattle upon a thousand hills.' 'If you think you are benefiting me,' says God in effect, 'when you bring your bulls and goats and your birds, I know all the fowls of the mountains: and the wild beasts of the field are mine. If I were hungry (which is impossible because I am God and because I am Spirit, but if I were hungry) I would not tell thee: for the world is mine, and the fulness thereof. Will I eat the flesh of bulls, or drink the blood of goats?' You see, these people had become so debased that they really thought that they were conferring a benefit upon God by taking their burnt offerings and sacrifices to the Temple. They were, as it were, patronising God. That is the psalmist's analysis of their misunderstanding and misinterpretation of the use of burnt offerings and sacrifices.

But let me translate this into its modern setting, let me put on the modern garb. Here it is—a purely formal religion. It may surprise some of you to hear me, a Christian preacher, saying a thing like this, but I am almost persuaded that the chief problem today is not the problem of people who say that there is no God and who are outside in the world. It is the problem of people who go to the house of God in a purely mechanical manner. They go there—why? Because it is the thing to do, it is a part of the social round. They attend a church as a matter of duty. It is like putting on a certain suit in order to go to a place of worship on Sunday morning only, and it is done with a pure formality; it is entirely external.

God knows, we have all been guilty of this, we may still be guilty. Why do we come to God's house? What really is the character of our worship when we come to analyse it? Is it not true that, in exactly the same way as God's people of old, we feel that we gain merit by doing it? There are probably thousands of people who still go to church on Sunday morning and then they are finished; they have done it, as it were, so they can go and do anything else they like now, write the family letters, play their games, read the Sunday newspapers, look at the television, watch some exciting thing here or there—anything. They have been to church on Sunday morning, and that is all. That was exactly the position of these children of Israel. It was formal, it was mechanical, but they felt it was meritorious. So it is now. 'We are the good people,' they say, 'not like those outsiders who don't believe in God, *we* go to a place of worship.'

What a terrible thing this position is! It is, in a sense, let me repeat, ten times worse than the person who is outside and who says, 'There is no God at all,' to go to God and to His house in a formal manner only and indeed almost with the idea that we are conferring some benefit upon Him. How nice of us! How good of us to have gone to a place of worship! We preen and pride ourselves on it. We go just once on Sunday and that is enough. And somehow or other we have been almost patronising God in our spirits. That was the trouble with those people and, alas, this whole attitude and spirit is much too common. 'Why should I be bothered?' says somebody. We have to be persuaded to worship God; we have to be persuaded to go to His house and we feel we are making a great sacrifice when we go there.

Those are the people I am dealing with. God forbid that there should be any such person reading these words at this moment. What does it mean? Well, let me sum it all up in this way: the trouble with such people is that they are entirely in control of their religion. *They* are at the centre, and God is just being considered and put into His place. It is what they think about God that is the truth about Him, and they will worship God in their way, when and how they want to; they are absolutely in control. They determine everything—*'Thou thoughtest.'* That is the first charge against these people; they do certain things in an appallingly wrong manner.

But the second principle is this: consider the things that these people fail to do. First of all, though they talk about God and declare His statutes and take His covenants in their mouths; though they believe in God and are tremendously interested in Him; in spite of all this, they fail to realise who and what God is. You know, this is the whole trouble in connection with religion; this is the key to all our problems and all our difficulties, every single one of them.

The fundamental trouble in the world today is just that one failure. There are people who tell us that they are in grave difficulties about certain doctrines of the Christian faith. They say, 'I'd like to be a Christian, I'd like to believe your gospel, but I can't.' They say, too, 'You ask me to believe this doctrine of sin, but I can't believe in it.' And do you know why? 'Well,' they say, 'I look into myself and I really don't feel that I'm a sinner, and I don't believe that the world is as bad as the Bible makes out, I don't

think people are as bad as you preach, or as some of you Christians say that we are, I just don't believe it.' So the reason why
they cannot believe the doctrine of sin is because they do not
know God; it is because they do not understand who and what
God is.

You will never make yourself feel that you are a sinner, because
there is a mechanism in you as a result of sin which will always be
defending you against every accusation. We are all on very good
terms with ourselves, and we can always put up a good case for
ourselves even if we try to make ourselves feel that we are sinners;
we will never do it. There is only one way to know that we are
sinners, and that is to have some dim, glimmering conception of
God.

Look at these men in the Bible who came anywhere near Him.
Listen to Isaiah when he has the vision of God; he says, 'I am
undone!' because 'I am a man of unclean lips' (Is 6:5). He does not
know what to do with himself. Why? It is because of the holiness
of God. It is the same with Moses, it is the same with every one of
them. That, you see, is the difficulty that people find with the
doctrine of sin; it is their failure to know the truth about God. And
it is exactly the same with the doctrine of the atonement. People
say, 'You know, I would like to be a Christian, but I can't believe
what you ask me to believe. You tell me that Christ has died for my
sins and that if He hadn't, I would be punished to all eternity. I
just can't take that. It is immoral, it seems to me; I am trying to
believe it, but I can't grasp it.'

Oh, my dear friend, there is only one trouble with you if that is
your problem. It is that you have no conception of the righteousness, the justice and the immutability of God, or of His holiness. If
you knew what the Bible means when it says, 'Our God is a
consuming fire' (Heb 12:29); if you knew what it means when it
says that He is 'dwelling in the light which no man can approach
unto' (1 Tim 6:16); if you have just begun to realise all that means
and that God cannot go back on His word, then you would see the
absolute necessity of the atonement.

And so, you see, all these difficulties with all the doctrines
eventually come back to this one great, central difficulty: our

ignorance of God. And the people who talk like this about God so glibly, who take this theoretical interest in Him and who believe that they are patronising Him and pleasing Him by doing their mechanical actions; the trouble with them is that they do not know Him.

What then should they know? Well, here is the answer. Listen to the first statement in this psalm: 'The mighty God...the Lord.' The psalmist starts with three names of God: *El*, *Elohim* and *Jehovah*. These names mean this: the almighty one has spoken; the only one who is the proper object of worship has spoken. The almighty God, *Elohim*; the Lord, *Jehovah*, the self-existent, the eternal one. That is the one about whom we are speaking.

Now, may the Holy Spirit of God enable me to open your eyes and your understanding that we may all grasp this. Oh, the way we speak about God! We have all done it; I have done it myself. I have been one of a company discussing religion and God and theology, and there we all sat in armchairs, smoking either cigarettes or pipes, and we were discussing God. The amazing thing is that God tolerates us at all and that He does not wipe us out of existence! You remember what happened to Moses at the burning bush. He said, 'What is this? This is an interesting phenomenon, I'm going to investigate it,' and he was on the point of approaching when the Voice came out of the bush and addressed him, saying, 'Stand back! Put off thy shoes from off thy feet. For the place whereon thou standest is holy ground' (Ex 3:5).

If you and I but realised the real nature and being of God, then we would stop speaking. We would stop mouthing these things and making our declarations. With Job of old, when he really came into God's presence, we would put our hands upon our mouths. We would be ashamed of ourselves for having spoken 'unadvisedly with our lips', and we would be silent before Him. And that is the only right and true and appropriate attitude.

If you want to know anything about God and to be blessed by Him, then you do not start by speaking about Him, nor by thinking what you want to think about what God ought to be like, or about what God ought to do. You just stop in silence, and you wait and you listen, and you adore and you look up. 'The mighty God, even Jehovah, hath spoken.'

Have you ever realised who God is? Everything in connection with religion is about Him. Christ came into the world and died. Why? To bring us to God. It is all about God. It is not some comfortable feeling that you and I have to get; it is not having your body healed or a thousand and one other things. The whole object of Christ and His death upon the cross, His burial and His resurrection is to bring us to God. And the ultimate test of our profession of the Christian faith is our thoughts about God, our attitude in His presence, our reverence and godly fear because our God is a consuming fire.

The second thing that the psalmist says is that the people failed to obey Him and to keep His laws. That is the whole point of verse 16 and following. They do not order their lives and conversation aright. They are called 'the wicked' because they declare His statutes and take His covenants in their mouths, but they hate His instruction and cast His words behind them. They do the things they want to do, they join the thief or the adulterer; they are interested in evil and they speak evil about one another—the whole horror of it all! 'Thou givest thy mouth to evil, and thy tongue frameth deceit. Thou sittest and speaketh against thy brother.' They malign their fellow church members and they say things about one another. They mouth about God and His wrath, but this is what they actually do—the wicked! They do not keep the laws of God, they do not live according to them and you see what that means.

Why has God given His laws? What is the purpose of the Ten Commandments? Did God promulgate them on Mount Sinai simply to provide a subject for discussion in a debating society? Are they simply intellectual matters on which you and I express our opinions? What is the purpose and the object of His statutes? There is only one answer: they are not to be discussed, they are to be kept. They are not even to be applauded, they are to be applied. God does not want our opinion upon His laws. There is no credit to us if we stand against the modern tendency which goes lower and lower and just say, 'No, no, the law of God says this and that.'

That is not what God wants; He wants us to keep these laws. We are to worship Him and nobody and nothing else: not our country, not our possessions, not our children, not anything—it must be God alone; there are to be no idols. We are not to bow down to any graven image. We are to honour God's day. We must not kill. We must not steal. We must not commit adultery. We are not to discuss these things, we must not do them. God has given His laws and His statutes that they might be kept and lived and practised. God is to be glorified by our obedience to Him and our honouring of His holy laws. That was His purpose in giving them.

Then the next thing that these people failed to realise is a tremendous and appalling thing; they failed to realise that God is the Judge and that He will judge: 'the heavens shall declare His righteousness: for God is Judge Himself.'

But let me expound it to you in terms of verse 21. Here were these people, talking about God, talking about His laws and His statutes, taking their burnt offerings and sacrifices and then forgetting all about Him and living according to their own ideas and plans and notions. Then for a moment they felt a little fear because there was something within them, their conscience, which spoke to them and told them that this was wrong. They did have a theoretical knowledge of the law and they wondered what was going to happen. But nothing happened. Now, when we all begin to sin consciously we expect something to happen to us, do we not? We have heard of Ananias and Sapphira, how they lied to the Holy Ghost and then were struck dead and we start with a feeling that, because we have done a certain thing, God will strike us or do something to us. But then nothing happens. And then, this is the result: 'These things hast thou done, and I kept silence; thou thoughtest that I was altogether such an one as thyself.'

How well we all know that! It works out like this: we begin to argue that because God does not strike at once, He will not strike at all. We think that God is as we are. Perhaps we may have said to a child, 'If you do that, I will have to punish you.' Then the child did it, but we did not punish him. Perhaps we forgot all about it, perhaps somebody came in to see us, and we got so animated in the conversation that we forgot all about it, and the child who was expecting to be punished, sneaked into bed and nothing happened. So we say, 'Perhaps God is like that; perhaps He just forgets. We thought we were going to be punished but nothing has happened.' 'I kept silence, thou thoughtest I was just such another as thyself.'

Or we may have thought, 'Perhaps God hasn't seen it at all; perhaps because I did it in secret He knows nothing about it, or if He does, He's forgotten, or in any case, He will do nothing about it. God, of course has given His laws, but we often lay down the law and do nothing about it, and God is like us perhaps. He has given the law, but He has not applied it at once and He probably never will. Nothing will happen to us. Carry on! All is well; God is love and everything will be all right.'

This is the most terrible mistake that a human being can ever make. Listen:

> Thou thoughtest that I was altogether
> such as one as thyself:
> but I will reprove thee,
> and set them in order before thine eyes.
> Now consider this, ye that forget God,
> lest I tear you in pieces,
> and there be none to deliver.

'Thou thoughtest that I was altogether such an one as thyself.' But God is not like us. He is eternally and absolutely different. He is just and righteous and holy and eternal and without change, and what He has said, He will most surely perform. He knows all about us and our every action, nothing is hid from His sight. If you fly up into heaven, He will be there; go to hell, He will be there. Travel eastwards, you cannot get away; go to the West, He is there before you. Go where you like, try as you will; you cannot hide from Him. He is everywhere. He knows everything: 'I will set them in order before thine eyes.'

There is a day coming, says the Book of Revelation, when 'the books' will be opened. These are the books that contain the record of every single deed that you and I and everybody who has ever lived, or ever will live in this world, has ever done. Everything that we do and think and say is known unto God: 'All things are naked and opened unto the eyes of him with whom we have to do' (Heb 4:13). The man outside says he does not believe all this and he is consistent, because he does not believe in God. But I am talking to people who say they believe in God. So if you believe in Him, you must believe this, otherwise you are a fool in your self-contradiction. If God is God, He knows all about us, every one of us, and He will never forget because He cannot forget. It is all known to Him; He will set it out in order before us. We shall have to give an account of the deeds done in the body, every one of us. This is the doctrine of the Bible from beginning to end, and these people forget that.

And then, next, they fail to worship God and to praise Him. 'Offer unto God thanksgiving and pay thy vows unto the most High' (v 14). 'Whoso offereth praise glorifieth me,' says God (v 23). And it is here that we come to one of the most glorious aspects of this biblical message. You see, what God wants is our hearts. He does not want our burnt offerings and sacrifices as such; He does not want our theoretical and intellectual interest in himself; He does not want us just to be arguing theology. No, no! He wants our hearts! He does not merely want our opinions, our actions. He can be independent of it all—'the cattle upon a thousand hills' belong to God and He knows all. The 'fowls of the mountains; and the wild beasts of the field' are His. The world is His, 'and the fulness thereof'. No, there is nothing you and I can give to God, but there is this one thing that He does ask of us: 'My son, give me thine heart.'

Do you remember how our Lord put it one afternoon in answering the question of the lawyer, 'What is the first and the greatest commandment of the law?' He replied, ' "Thou shalt love the Lord thy God with all thy heart and with all thy soul and with all thy mind and with all thy strength" ' (Mk 12:30). He does not want your mind only, He wants your heart and soul and strength. He wants *you*. What God wants of every one of us is that our whole attitude to Him should be right. He wants our praise, He wants our thanksgiving, He wants our worship. Some people can write a cheque for a thousand pounds and not miss it, God does not want that if their heart is not given to Him. You can give the whole world to God, but if you do not give yourself it is of no value, it is no good at all; God will be displeased with you and He will call you 'wicked'. He wants worship, He wants praise and He wants the homage of the heart.

So, let me put that in a final principle. The real failure of these people is their failure to surrender to God. It is their failure to realise their utter and absolute dependence upon Him. 'Offer unto God thanksgiving; and pay thy vows unto the most High'—and then if you call upon Him in the day of trouble, He will deliver you. Here it is, in the last verse: 'Whoso offereth praise glorifieth me; and to him that ordereth his conversation aright will I shew the salvation of God.' You see, it just comes to this. God wants us to realise who He is, and to realise our utter dependence upon Him. He does not want our opinions and our external, mechanical actions; He wants us to call upon Him, to seek His salvation. Our Lord makes this point in the parable of the Pharisee and the Publican who went up to the Temple to pray. The Pharisee steps forward and says, 'God, I thank thee that I am not as other men are, extortioners, unjust, adulterous, or even as this Publican. I fast twice in the week, I give tithes of all that I possess' (Lk 18:11–12). 'That's the sort of man I am, how wonderful!'

The other man, far back by the door, beating his breast, could not so much as lift up his face to look at God because he was so ashamed, and this is all he said, 'God, be merciful to me, a sinner.' 'I tell you,' says Christ, 'this man went down to his house justified rather than the other.' That is what God wants: that we shall so realise who and what He is, and see our smallness and our insignificance and our sinfulness to such an extent, that we put our hands upon our mouths. We stop doing things and relying upon them and we just say, 'God, have mercy upon me! Show me thy salvation, deliver me!' And He will answer us and say, 'I have already done so. I sent my only Son into the world to deliver you. I sent Him even to the death of the cross. I laid your sins and iniquities upon Him and I smote Him with the stripes that should come to you and which you so richly deserved. I have done that!

There is my salvation, I am showing it to you! Believe it, receive it and then begin and continue and go on for the rest of your life in glorifying me, in praising my name.'

My friends, it comes to this: what is your attitude in the presence of God? What do you believe about God? Is your whole life centred in Him? If you believe in God, that will be the case. There is nothing more awful and reprehensible than to talk about Him, and then to forget all about Him, and to live as if He were not there at all. Are you calling upon God for salvation? Have you seen your desperate need of Him? Do you know that you will have to face Him in the Judgement? And perhaps there will be, as it were, a tape-recording played back to you of all you have said about God and how you have spoken about Him and His laws and declared His statutes; it will all be played back to you. And then it will be read out to you, the things that you have done, the life you have lived, your self-centredness, your selfishness, the fact that your whole life was not surrendered to God and lived to His glory and to His praise.

It is a tremendous thing to say you believe in God; look at the implications. If you really believe in Him, these are the truths. He is the Almighty God, Jehovah, the Judge before whom everyone of us will have to stand. Are you humbled before God? 'Humble yourselves under the mighty hand of God'—and if you do so, I promise you—'He will exalt you' (1 Pet 5:6). 'Believe on the Lord Jesus Christ and thou shalt be saved' (Acts 16:31).   Amen.

3 *THE SPARROW AND THE SWALLOW*

How amiable are thy tabernacles, O Lord of hosts!
My soul longeth, yea, even fainteth for the
courts of the Lord: my heart and my flesh
crieth out for the living God.
Yea, the sparrow hath found an house,
and the swallow a nest for herself, where
she may lay her young, even thine altars,
O Lord of hosts, my King and my God.
Blessed are they that dwell in thy house:
They will be still praising thee.
(PS. 84:1–3)

A S WE CONSIDER THESE verses from Psalm 84 together, I want
to deal in particular with the message of the third verse:
'Yea, the sparrow hath found an house, and the swallow a
nest for herself, where she may lay her young, even thine altars, O
Lord of hosts, my King and my God.' We shall study this message
because this 84th Psalm is written by a man who tells us that the
greatest thing in life is to enjoy the blessings of the godly life.

To him this is more important than anything else, he would
give the whole world for it. It means everything to him, not only
when all is going well, but still more when things seem to be so
conspiring against him as almost to drive him to despair. 'There is
nothing,' he says, 'in the whole world that is comparable to this.'
So he keeps on offering up his praise: 'How amiable are thy
tabernacles, O Lord of hosts,' he begins; and he ends with the

words: 'Blessed is the man that trusteth in thee' (v 12), and you might well translate that word 'blesséd' as 'happy'. His whole theme, therefore, is that there is no happiness on earth which is in any way comparable to that of the man or woman who knows God.

So then, the great question for us is: are we able to say that kind of thing? Have we shared the experience of the psalmist? Can we say that as far as we are concerned, the loving-kindness of God is better than life itself? That is how David puts it in another psalm. Are the courts of God's house amiable to us? Which is just another way of saying: is this communion with God the supreme thing in the whole of our life and existence and experience here in the world?

It is, then, in order that we may discover how to arrive at that that we are considering the message of this great psalm; because this man tells us that there are certain things which are absolute essentials if we are to enjoy it even as he did. In the first two verses, he deals with the two great preliminaries. It is no use going any further until we are clear about these. Religion, finally, is a question of knowing God. It is not primarily a matter of living, nor is it just a question of a good life or of doing good. No, the essence of religion is to know God. You notice how he keeps on impressing that upon us: 'O Lord of hosts, my King and my God,' 'Blessed is the man whose strength is in thee.'

And then he is careful to tell us, wise teacher as he is, the only way in which that knowledge can be obtained. He says, 'I have obtained it at *the altars* and there is no other way.' There is no way to know God except through Jesus Christ and Him crucified. This is the centre and beginning of Christianity. Man must know God. Well, there is only one way, and Christ said so Himself repeatedly: 'I am the way, the truth and the life. No man cometh unto the Father but by me' (Jn 14:6). That is His own claim. So if you think you can arrive at God without Him, you are already denying the first principles.

We have not only got to come through Him, we must also realise that we come through His broken body and through His shed blood. There is only one living way which has been made for us and that is the way upon the cross on Calvary's hill. The only thing that brings us into the presence of God, says the author of the Epistle to the Hebrews, is 'the blood of Jesus' (Heb 10:19).

The second thing we see in this psalm is that we must realise that it is this objective truth about God which matters supremely. We must not rest on our own feelings and experiences and moods and states. There are many things that can give us happy feelings, but a happy feeling is not of necessity a knowledge of God. It does result from a true knowledge of God, but, according to this man, unless we can know and rely upon the character of God in all its greatness and its majesty, we really have no foundation.

There, then, are the preliminary considerations and we must realise and accept them. But there is also, according to the psalmist, one other thing which we must also realise, and that is the truth about ourselves. There are two things which are always the two poles, as it were, of Christian truth. Christian truth is a kind of ellipse and there is one focus—God; but there is this other focus—man; and if we are to enjoy the experience of this writer we must be as right about man as we are about God.

He starts with God, and we must start with Him, but it is not enough, because we must then come down and look at ourselves. This is the very essence of Christian experience. We must be right in our thinking about God, but we must be equally right in our thinking about ourselves. Read the lives of the saints, the biographies of men and women who have trod this earth, who have lived in it as you and I do, who have been able to conquer life and to master it and to rejoice in spite of all adversity, and who have sung the praises of God. And when you have read them, you will always find that they are men and women who have discovered certain things about themselves. It is invariable.

What, then, are these things? Well, fortunately for us, the psalmist describes them in the form of a picture and it is a picture which really explains itself. 'The sparrow,' he says, 'hath found an house, and the swallow a nest for herself, where she may lay her young.' Now there are some people who completely misinterpret this statement by taking it to mean that the psalmist is more or less complaining. He says, 'Ah, the sparrow and the swallow have been able to build a nest on thine altars in the tabernacle, while I am far away from the tabernacle and I cannot find this place.' Such a view, of course, is monstrous. You could never have a nest on the altar where animals' bodies were broken up and then burnt; it is impossible! That is no place of safety for a sparrow or for a swallow!

No, what the psalmist is saying, in effect, is this: 'I'm like a sparrow, I'm like a swallow, but I'm like the sparrow that has found a house for herself and I'm like the swallow that has found a nest where she may lay her young. And thank God, the place where I have found the right position and all the right conditions for making my nest and laying my young is thine altars, "O Lord of hosts, my King and my God." Here is the secret: it was only when I came to see myself as a sparrow and as a swallow that I really discovered my need and then went to God and found my answer and my supply.'

You will find this truth worked out in a more doctrinal and theological manner in many places in the New Testament. To take one at random, our Lord said that He had 'not come to call the righteous but sinners to repentance' (Mt 9:13). He also said, 'They that are whole have no need of the physician, but they that are sick' (Mk 2:17); or again, 'The Son of Man is come to seek and to save that which was lost' (Lk 19:10). In other words, you will always find this element; men and women must realise their need, and the only people who know what it is to enjoy the blessings of Christian salvation are those who have already discovered that need. The tragedy, ultimately, of so many, indeed of all outside Christ, is that they have never really seen their need. That is why they have never seen the need of Christ; that is why they do not fly to Him as Saviour; they have never seen themselves.

Let us follow this man as he brings out in this wonderful picture the needs of the soul, the realisations that drive people to Christ and make them flee to Him for salvation. There are certain things which always characterise truly Christian men and women. The first is that they have become aware of their own smallness. A sparrow; a swallow. A sparrow is one of the smallest birds and the psalmist is saying here, in effect, 'I came to see that I was just like a little sparrow or swallow.'

Nobody, you see, is a Christian without realising the immensity and greatness of life and no one comes to realise that, of course, without thinking. The trouble with all of us, in this world, is that we tend to be absorbed in life, and life sees to it that we never are given a moment to think and to meditate and to ponder. We just take things for granted and we go on. But then suddenly a man or woman begins to think; they begin to discover their own smallness, and it has led them to feel that they are but as sparrows.

Let me explain a little further. Think of this vast universe in which we are situated. Now, there are many people at the present time who argue that the discoveries of science, especially during this twentieth century, have unfolded to us this mysterious universe in which we live. Scientists talk about billions and billions of miles; they talk about all these vast constellations which are almost endless in number, and, these people say, 'God is at the back of it all.' So then their immediate deduction is, 'Well, who am I in such a vast universe?' The psalmist expresses it so clearly for us in the eighth Psalm. He says, 'When I consider thy heavens the work of thy fingers, the moon and the stars which thou hast ordained.' Then his response is: 'What is man that thou art mindful of him?' He says, 'The thing is incredible!'

And there are many people who have faced the Christian salvation like that today and who dismiss it and deride it. They say, 'You Christians are too introspective, too self-centred; you're exaggerating your own importance. Who are you that the almighty and eternal God could be interested in you as an individual?'

There are many people who deny and reject Christianity for that reason. They say, 'I'm nobody,' and then they begin to think of other things. They think of all the teeming masses in this world. 'And what is the individual?' they ask. 'What is the value of an individual? Is he anything more than cannon fodder? When millions of people may suddenly be put to death by the explosion of one bomb, who am I? And is it right for me to think about myself? Is there any place for me?' So men and women are overawed by the immensity of creation and by the huge mass of humanity.

Yet, on the other hand, we are aware of ourselves as individuals, we are aware of an identity. I have my own life and yet how small and how insignificant it seems to be; who can be concerned about it, what hope is there for me? Many today are appalled and overwhelmed by that consideration. They say, 'What is man, after all, but just a speck in a great lump? Is he anything but a little cog in a great wheel? Does anything matter except the wheel? Is there any place for the individual?' So they have become aware at one and the same time of the immensity of it all and of their own smallness and their own apparent insignificance. The sparrow; the swallow.

Now, what I am anxious to emphasise is that as I understand the teaching of the Bible, no man or woman has ever become a Christian without having just some sense of that. Here they are, as it were, a little focus in this vast business of life, conscious of their unutterable smallness, and they are tempted to think that they are so small that they are finally insignificant.

But let me go on. In addition to this sense of smallness and insignificance, there is also a sense of 'homelessness' and this is something which the psalmist brings out very prominently. 'Yea,' he says, 'the sparrow hath found an house'—at last. The sparrow had been looking for this house for some time. And the swallow, in the same way, has at last found 'a nest for herself where she may lay her young.' She had been flying about and looking for it; that place seemed hopeful and she went there, but no, it was not right, so she tried another...and the poor swallow was beginning to think that she would never find a place at all, and so did the little sparrow; but at last 'the sparrow hath found an house,' and the swallow a place where she can build her little nest and bring up her young in it.

Now all this is, again, a wonderful picture of a feeling that comes inevitably to every man or woman who finally becomes a Christian. It is this sense of homelessness or, to put it in other words, a great sense of restlessness. Here we are in the world, a world which we have not made. Nor have we made ourselves, we just find ourselves here. We become aware of its greatness and of other forces and factors, and we begin to ask certain questions.

What is life? What are we doing here? Where are we going? Is there any sense or meaning in it? Is there any final object and purpose to it all? And the moment you begin to face these questions you are aware of this restlessness, this homelessness.

The modern world is full of it. I could illustrate it at very great length. You see, it is because of this very restlessness that men and women are clutching at almost anything today in order to try and get a certain amount of peace and rest. That is why in an age like this the cults are popular. For the old comfortable philosophy has been shattered by the two world wars. There was a time before 1914 when, on paper at any rate, a very good case could be made out for the fact that life had at last outgrown its growing pains and that man was settling down. It was believed that there was an era of great prosperity which probably would go on for ever and ever and that people, getting to know one another, would cease to hate one another and would banish war, and all would be happy together and life would be harmonious.

There seemed to be a great deal to be said in those days for such reasoning, but all that has gone now. That illusion has been shattered. Our whole life has been rocking and shaking and we do not know where we are. We are seeking for rest and for peace. There is a restlessness within. You are aware, are you not, of the new diseases that are coming heavily upon us? As so-called miracle drugs cure the old infections and diseases one after another, so these other diseases are coming in. Many of them are diseases of stress and strain. Diseases of the heart, diseases like blood pressure, taut nerves, anxiety neuroses and all these things, how common they are becoming! It is even becoming a great problem for the government and for the State; where can all these patients be housed, what are we to do with them?

Now, all this is a manifestation of this very restlessness which the psalmist describes so graphically to us. He says, 'I began to feel like a little sparrow or a swallow. I could not find a house for myself. I wished I could have found some place where I could have built my nest in safety and where I could have laid the eggs and brought up my young, but I could not find one and I was flying hither and thither and becoming weary and tired and I did not

know what to do with myself. And what could I do? I flew help-
lessly, seeking and searching, but I could not find.' Have you
known anything about that?

You see, up until a certain point we do not think about these
things at all, do we? We just eat and drink, we go on from day to
day and we never give a thought to any of them. But suddenly
something will force us to do so—an illness or an accident or a
death or some calamity. Something happens and we begin to say,
'Isn't there a place of rest? Isn't there somewhere where I can find a
quiet heart? Isn't there some philosophy that can give me tran-
quillity?' So we read the novels and they do not satisfy us because
we see through them. We say we are drugging ourselves intellectually, so we may try drink, we may try pleasure; we may take up
politics or go in for social activities; we may take up a course on
philosophy. We may take up a thousand and one things, art and
music. But still the restlessness continues.

These things seem to pass by and they leave 'the world to
darkness and to me'. The dance ends, the play ends, the music
ends and you are left alone and you do not know quite where you
are. And you are wondering what you are and what you are
destined for and what it is all about. You say, 'I would give the
whole world if only I could find some house, some resting place
where there would be an end to all this searching and seeking.' If
you read the confessions of a man like St Augustine he will tell you
that this is what it is all about. He was a brilliant man, but great
brain as he was, he could not find this place of rest. He was like the
little swallow, flickering, flying hither and thither thinking he had
got it and then finding he had not. He tried another idea and again
it was an illusion and on and on it went. And no man or woman
has ever become a true Christian unless they have known this
sense of restlessness, this feeling of homelessness. People have an
instinct within them—the homing instinct, if you like—which
tells them that there is a place if they could but find it. But this they
cannot do.

The third characteristic of Christian men and women, those
who have come to enjoy the blessings of religion as this psalmist
enjoyed them, is that at the same time, and for the reasons that I

have been giving, they become aware of their own helplessness, their own defencelessness. These little birds know that; they know by a kind of instinct that they have certain enemies. There are larger birds; there are cats and all the other beasts—things that accompany them in creation and which are all watching them so that they are concerned to find a place of safety, somewhere beyond the reach of these enemies that are ever threatening them.

Have you ever watched a sparrow on a lawn? There he is, pecking away at something, and yet if there is the slightest movement he jumps at once. He sees behind, he looks in front, he watches the side, have you ever seen a more nervous creature? His instinct is full of this sense of alarm and self-protection. At any moment some predatory beast may descend upon him and he flits away: the defencelessness, the smallness, the utter helplessness of these little birds!

Now, the tragedy of so many lives today is that men and women are not aware of these enemies. But the moment they are on the way to being Christians it is because they are becoming aware of their complete helplessness and defencelessness. What are these things that attack us? Let us look at some of them.

Many people have gone through life without thinking at all until they have suddenly been stricken by an illness. I have watched it so often. There are people who have even scoffed at me and my profession of the Christian faith and who have not hesitated in various ways to tell me that they think I am a fool. Everything was all right, work or profession going well, no shortage of money, wife and children happy, everything perfect and they would regard me or any other Christian as just being morbid and introspective. 'Why not enjoy life?' they said. 'Why live that miserable existence?' They were not aware, you see, of the enemies that were ready to pounce. There they were on their lawns, as it were, pecking away at their food and enjoying it tremendously, not aware of all the gathering enemies. Suddenly one strikes! Illness, accident....

Take a man like Doctor Thomas Chalmers, one of the great preachers and teachers in Scotland in the last century. That was his position even as a 'Christian preacher' for ten years. He really wasn't one, of course, because he did not know this gospel, though he thought he did and was perfectly happy. He was a man who preached 'scientific' sermons, and he said that it was finding himself on a bed for ten months, helpless and stricken, lying flat on his back, that awakened him. The enemy! And he found he had got nothing, nothing to sustain him. He was defenceless and quite helpless.

An accident, too, may weaken us. Death may visit our family or threaten us, and we become aware of how small we are, how frail and utterly helpless we are. These things come and we have no reply. We can do nothing at all about them and we do not know what to do nor where to turn.

Then, of course, as we become more spiritual in our under-standing, we become aware of the onslaughts that are made upon us by the world, by the flesh and by the devil. We start off in life, perhaps, with high ideals and wonderful visions. 'Others,' we say, 'have failed in the past, but that is no reason why we should fail.' We are confident that we can handle ourselves in the situation, that we can go on and that all will be well. But the attack comes; suddenly we have lost something precious which we had had until that moment and now it is gone. Chastity, purity, morality, honesty—certain things which we had priced so highly—they are gone! They have been taken from us. We are bereft of them. The enemy has come and has attacked and we did not seem to have any means of defence, no means of protecting ourselves from the onslaught.

Ah you see, it is only those who begin to realise that they have got sin within them who realise that their very nature is twisted and perverted. They see that there is something wrong and foul in their own hearts and the power of sin within them and without them. They realise that in addition to that, the whole world is set against them, that the flesh is militating against them and that the devil is behind it all. They begin to see all these things and they are terrified, afraid of themselves.

They no longer say, 'Let any temptation come and I can stand up to it.' They discover that there is the most dangerous thing in the world, that when they thought they were strong, they suddenly went down. They went out of the house determined never to fall again, but they had fallen before they knew where they were. They begin to realise how helpless they are, how utterly defenceless. They are like that little sparrow; that tiny swallow. These other creatures are so mighty and strong.

Have you come to this realisation? Have you known anything yet of the moral struggle? Have you known what it is to fight with all your might and yet go down with all these enemies that are attacking you?

But that brings us to the last illustration, and it is one of the most marvellous of all. 'Yea,' says the psalmist, 'the sparrow hath found an house, and the swallow a nest for herself, where she may lay her young.' These little birds have a wonderful instinct. They do not understand it intellectually but they do understand it instinctively and intuitively. They know that the most marvellous thing that they can ever do is to bring up their young; to lay the eggs, to sit upon them and to hatch them, to rear the fledgelings, and to guard them and to feed them until the point when they have so developed and matured that they can fly over the edge of the nest themselves and begin their own life. To the little bird there is nothing that is more precious than her young and that is why she is looking for a house or for a place where she may build her nest.

And so, the ultimate secret of every godly Christian, the real secret of this psalmist as he puts it so plainly here, is that he has come at last to realise that the most priceless thing in life is his soul. This is a psalm of King David: a mighty warrior, a man who slew Goliath; a man who could boast of many a victory; one who had conquered his enemies; the greatest king that Israel ever knew, and one who enjoyed great pomp and ceremony and many things about which men like to boast.

But, 'No,' says David, 'I have discovered that the most priceless possession I have, though I am a great king, is my soul. There is nothing more precious than this. All these things I will have to leave behind me, but there is that within me which is imperishable. There is this within me which goes on for all eternity. It is the thing that God has put into me, that which God breathed into man so that he "became a living soul" ' (Gen 2:7). It is the thing that stamps men and women as being made in the image of God. 'My soul! The most precious thing of all, that is what I want to safeguard and protect.'

In the New Testament, the Apostle Paul says the same thing. This is how he puts it: 'I know whom I have believed and am persuaded that He is able to keep that which I have committed unto Him against that day' (2 Tim 1:12). 'It is all right,' says Paul, in effect, 'things are going against me, but I am perfectly happy. Why? Because I have committed my soul and its safe-keeping to God and Christ and I know whatever may happen to me, He will "keep that which I have committed unto Him" until that great Day of Judgement. It is safe.'

Do you remember how the Lord Jesus Christ put it? He says in Matthew 6:25–34, 'Do not waste your time in worrying about what you will eat or drink or how you will be clothed. All the nations of the world are interested in these things; it is the Gentiles who go after things like that.' So what are we to be worried about? Here it is: 'Seek ye first the kingdom of God and His righteousness; and all these things shall be added unto you.' Oh yes, the body is important but not as important as the soul. What of your soul? 'What shall it profit a man if he shall gain the whole world, and lose his own soul? Or what shall a man give in exchange for his soul?' (Mk 8:36). 'Ah,' says David, here in Psalm 84, 'I'm like the little sparrow and the swallow. I have the most priceless possession. In their case it is the young, in mine it is the soul and I have awakened to this. My soul! Where can I put it that I may know it is safe with all these enemies attacking and life being what it is? Is there no place where I may know that my soul is safe for all eternity? That is what I want to know!' And these are the inevitable steps, are they not, that cause us all to seek and to search for salvation?

We are awakened to the fact that there is this soul within us; that when our bodies are mouldering in the grave becoming nothing, eaten by worms and disappearing, then this precious, priceless thing is going on—and will go on and on and on, and there is no end to it. The safety of the soul! That is the ultimate question. Have you become concerned about your soul? Are you alarmed about it? Have you realised that you will have to give to God an account of your soul and what you have done with it in this world?

Here then is the need that the psalmist depicts in terms of the sparrow and the swallow, but, thank God, he puts it positively: 'The sparrow *hath found* an house, and the swallow a nest for herself, where she may lay her young.' For this is the glory of the Christian gospel. It satisfies these four needs that I have been putting before you, and, in a most interesting way, our Lord seems to have expressed all this as a direct answer to the question of this psalm. 'Do not be worried and troubled about yourselves,' He said. 'Are not two sparrows sold for a farthing? And one of them shall not fall on the ground without your heavenly Father'. Then He added, 'Fear ye not therefore, ye are of more value than many sparrows' (Mt 10:29, 31). How much greater, He says, is your heavenly Father's concern and care for you?

Have you felt that you are just like a little sparrow in this world? Have you said to yourself, 'Well, I am such a little being and individual and entity, how can I matter in this great world?' My dear friend, let me give you the answer to that. You can read the story in Luke 8:43–48. One afternoon, our Lord was going, at the request of a great man called Jairus, to see his little daughter who had been very ill and who had died; and our Lord was hurrying along to the house to help him. Suddenly He was thronged by a great crowd. They were literally surrounding Him and pressing in upon Him so that they could scarcely move. Suddenly our Lord astonished His disciples by saying, 'Who touched me?' They turned to Him and said, 'Master! The multitude throng thee and press thee and sayest thou, "Who touched me?" ' (Lk 8:45). Why, man, a thousand people are touching you!

'No,' said Christ, 'somebody has touched me.' And a poor woman in the great crowd stepped forward, so ashamed of herself that she could scarcely lift up her head, and said, 'I touched you; or at least, I touched the hem of your garment.' Yes, she had touched Him in her desperate and awful need, and what I want to emphasise is that though He was thronged by a great crowd, the Son of

God knew of the individual, the lonely woman with the issue of blood whom nobody could heal, the one whom physicians could not help, the one isolated individual in the mob. 'Who touched me?' He knew.

And that is still the Lord Jesus Christ. Though you are one of the teeming millions in this world, and though the world would have you believe that you do not count and that you are but a speck in the mass, God says, 'I know you.'

We can see the same thing in another incident at the end of our Lord's life. There He was, dying on the cross, enduring that agony and shame, and the thief on one side said, 'Lord, remember me when thou comest into thy kingdom' (Lk 23:42)—and He did. He had time for him, though He was bearing the sins of the world and though He was experiencing things that you and I can never imagine. He was ready to listen to the isolated cry from this one man. He gave Himself to him, exclusively as it were, and gave him the glorious promise: 'This day, thou shalt be with me in paradise' (Lk 23:43).

This is the glorious message of the gospel. God who made the worlds and the stars and the constellations; this majestic Lord of Hosts whose name the psalmist celebrates seven times—do you know, He knows you! He is interested in us one by one. The sparrow; the swallow. Never again listen to that lie of the devil. You will find rest in this gospel. You will know that the Maker of heaven and earth is interested in you and has sent His Son into the world for you.

The same is true with our second problem; have you been seeking for rest? Well, I have already given the answer to that. The Son of God said, 'Come unto me, all ye that labour and are heavy-laden, and I will give you rest' (Mt 11:28). Have you tried the way of the world? Have you tried its pleasure, its laughter? Have you tried its philosophy, its thinking, its art and all its culture? Have you been trying to find some place where you can find rest for your soul?

There is only one place in the universe where you will find it, it is 'the altars'. It is only as you look at Him there dying on that cross that you will find rest and peace for yourself, for your soul. For He tells you here to stop striving; to make no more effort; it is not your seeking that will enable you to find—'Come unto me'. Just as you are, in your failure, in your helplessness; in your restlessness. 'Come to me and I will give you rest.' The sparrow has found a house and the swallow a place where she may make her nest and lay her young; the rest and the peace and the quiet that the gospel gives, the end of the seeking and the striving.

And then, of course, we have the safety and the protection. This man puts it in his own words: 'The Lord God is a sun and shield' (v 11). A light in the darkness; a shield to protect. Do you know anybody or anything that can protect you from the world, and the flesh and the devil? What can you do? What can the world do against these forces and powers that are trying to rob you and destroy your soul? There is only one answer again. The Lord Jesus Christ, using another analogy, comparing us to sheep and calling Himself the Good Shepherd, said, 'They shall never perish, neither shall any man pluck them out of my hand' (Jn 10:28). With the power of the Lord Jesus Christ through the Holy Spirit we can say,

> I need Thee every hour,
> Stay Thou nigh near by.

Why? Well:

> Temptations lose their power
> When Thou art nigh.

Annie Sherwood Hawkes

> I fear no foe with Thee at hand to bless

Henry Francis Lyte (1793–1847)

Oh, the strength and the power of Christ! He surrounds us: 'The name of the Lord is a strong tower' (Prov 18:10). 'For,' says the Apostle Paul, 'I am persuaded, that neither death, nor life, nor angels, nor principalities, nor powers, nor things present, nor things to come, nor height, nor depth, nor any other creature, shall be able to separate us from the love of God which is in Christ

Jesus, our Lord' (Rom 8:38–39). We are safe in the nest and no animal can come there. We are protected, we are surrounded; nothing and no one shall ever be able to separate us from that love.

And then, finally, the most priceless possession of all, the soul. Oh, where can I find safety for my soul? I have already been answering the question. There is only one place: 'The Son of Man is come to seek and to save that which was lost' (Lk 19:10). The Christ who died for us and for our sins, the Christ who saved us is the Christ who will continue to keep us. He will be with us 'to the river'. He has said, 'I will never leave thee nor forsake thee' (Heb 13:5). He will be with us in the river of death and beyond it. He will take us by the hand and present us 'faultless before the presence of [God's] glory with exceeding joy' (Jude :24).

> All the way, my Saviour leads me,
> What have I to ask beside?
> Can I doubt His tender mercy,
> Who through life has been my guide?
> Heavenly peace, divinest comfort,
> Here by faith in Him to dwell,
> For I know whate're befall me,
> Jesus doeth all things well.
>
> Fanny J. Crosby

He has died to save your soul and He will keep it safe through all eternity: 'Yea, yea, the sparrow hath found an house, and the swallow a nest where she may lay her young.' My friend, have you found it? Can you take your stand by the side of the psalmist and say, 'Yes, it is perfectly true, I have found my every need satisfied. The almighty God in heaven is interested in me and knows me. He is my God and I am His child and my soul is safe in the keeping of Christ.'

> A Sovereign Protector I have,
> Unseen, yet for ever at hand,
> Unchangeably faithful to save,
> Almighty to rule and command.

He smiles, and my comforts abound;
His grace, like the dew shall descend,
And walls of salvation surround,
The soul He delights to defend.

Augustus Toplady

Are you in the nest? Have you found the house? Can you say, 'Blessed is the man that trusteth in thee'? That is the way—enter into it!   Amen.

4 *THE HIGHWAY OF GOD*

> Blessed is the man whose strength is in thee;
> in whose heart are the ways of them.
> Who passing through the valley of Baca
> make it a well; the rain also filleth the pools.
> They go from strength to strength, every one
> of them in Zion appeareth before God.
> (PS 84:5–7).

WE ARE CONTINUING NOW with our study of this great eighty-fourth Psalm. Undoubtedly, let me remind you, it was King David himself who wrote it. The evidence, both internal and external, suggests that very strongly, and it was probably written by him at the time of the rebellion and insurrection of his own son Absalom, when David, thus suddenly taken unawares, had to escape from Jerusalem. There are graphic accounts of the whole incident in some of the historical books of the Old Testament, of how he literally had to flee for his life and found himself wandering through a wilderness, wondering what was going to happen to him and what his future would be.

As we have seen, his whole object in writing the psalm is just to report the fact that to him nothing matters so much in this life and in this world as true religion. It is a psalm which has been written to celebrate the glories and the benefits of the truly godly life. He keeps on saying that; he begins 'How amiable are thy tabernacles, O Lord of hosts,' and ends, 'O Lord of hosts, blessed is the man that trusteth in thee,' and in between he has said it many times. That is his one great theme, the thing that he is setting out to say, and he does it, of course, in order that he may encourage others to realise the importance of a life truly lived under God and under His blessing.

We have also seen how the psalmist is very careful to define what he means by true religion, because there are false notions around as to what is meant by religion. We all tend to think that we know by instinct what it is, but when you bring those various ideas and hold them in the light of biblical teaching, you discover at once how far they are from what is described here, and how many of them are entirely erroneous, indeed, the very exact opposite of what is revealed in these verses. So the psalmist starts with that and he lets us know at once that the essence, the whole of true religion, is to know God.

It is not simply to know things about Him, though that comes in. Nor is it to have certain views of life, though that is there too. The essence of religion is really and truly to know God so that you can address Him as this man does and say, 'My King and my God' (v 3). He tells us that 'his heart and his flesh crieth out for the living God', 'my soul longeth, yea, even fainteth for the courts of the Lord' (v 2). 'There is nothing,' he says, 'that matters finally, save this.' True religion is not just a matter of morality. That is included, but to make that the end of religion is to rob it of its central glory.

The psalmist has also, let me remind you, taken the precaution of telling us where and how exactly and only God can be known, and that place is at His 'altars'. We must start with this because it is no use going on to consider the benefits of Christianity unless we know something about Christ. It is at the altars that God is known, at the altar of sacrifice. There is no knowledge of God except in Jesus Christ and Him crucified. He is the sacrifice that is placed upon the altar: 'He hath made His soul an offering for sin' (Is 53:10). 'I am the way, the truth and the life' He says Himself. 'No man cometh unto the Father but by me' (Jn 14:6).

Then having thus laid down these fundamental and essential principles, David has gone on to describe to us something of the benefits and the blessings that ensue upon this knowledge of God and being in this place and position where God can bless us. In our last study we considered one of these things, and, incidentally, let me remind you of the fact that there is nothing that is so remarkable about this particular psalm as the way in which the psalmist uses his images and pictures and his analogies. A poet generally puts his truths in the form of pictures—he uses symbols—and this man was a poet, 'the sweet singer of Israel'.

So in his picture of the sparrow and the swallow, we saw that the first and one of the greatest and most blessed results of true religion and knowledge of God in Christ is that we are given a place of rest and safety for our souls.

But now we come on to another picture, and I think that the order in which the psalmist puts these things is not without significance. David's secret is that his strength is in God and not in himself. He has realised that God is the 'Lord of hosts'. He has discovered Him at the altar, and has found the way to Him. Yes, his strength is in God, but then this is what follows: 'Blessed is the man whose strength is in thee, in whose heart are ways.' Now, in this verse the translators of the Authorised Version have added the words 'of them' but they are not in the original. What the psalmist wrote was just 'in whose heart are ways', and the actual word he used for 'ways' means 'a made road'—a road that has been made deliberately. 'Blessed,' therefore, 'is the man who has made roads', or 'constructed thoroughfares' in his heart. Here again, then, the psalmist employs another very graphic picture. What does he mean by it and what is his teaching?

Let me put it like this, as a principle. The second great blessing that Christianity confers upon us is that it brings order into our lives. Let us follow David and use his picture. The heart of the person who is not a Christian is like a pathless wilderness. You may have read of settlers in early years in the United States or Canada or some other land that has only been discovered in the last few centuries, and you may have come across descriptions of how, when the settlers first arrived and landed, they found nothing but a kind of endless bush. There it was, virgin soil; a virgin country. No roads, no pathways, with trees and shrubs and all manner of herbs growing, and it was impossible for them to work their way through it. They could only move a few steps at a time and they had to beat a path out for themselves.

Now that is the kind of picture that the psalmist very clearly has in his mind here. The heart of the irreligious person is like that. It is uncharted wilderness which has never been cleared. There are no paths there and no highways—it has not been mapped out. Everything is tangled and mixed up, and then when you look at it you cannot see where you can go in any direction whatsoever.

Not only that, there are all these ups and downs, high hills and deep valleys. The whole area is in a kind of natural state. It has never been prospected and everything is in a state of utter confusion. Now it is very important that we should understand the psalmist's teaching at this point, because it is nothing but an accurate, detailed description of what we all are by nature as the result of the fall and as the result of the sin of the first man. Our lives, as they are untouched by the power of God, are simply like a pathless wilderness.

Let me explain. People who are not Christians really have no view or philosophy of life. That is the trouble with men and women who are outside the life of God. They have no clear ideas. They have never really thought things out. They are like a great uncharted territory, just a hopeless tangle, everything is mixed up and there is no rhyme nor reason. Everything is taken for granted, there is no order or system at all in their lives.

Am I being unfair? Well, I just ask you, if you are not a Christian, to look into your own mind or, perhaps, to talk to others. I ask you to read biographies and you will find that this is undoubtedly the case. Such people may adopt some temporary view but the vast majority do not even seem to do that. Life is just taken for granted and men and women live from hand to mouth and from day to day. There is no scheme, no understanding in their lives. To use the words of Matthew Arnold, they have never 'seen life steadily'; they have never 'seen it whole'.

In the same way, we can say of it that there is no plan in it and no purpose. The life of so many today is entirely aimless. They do not really live, they just exist. They do not sit down and say, 'What am I doing in this world? What am I altogether? What is man? What is life about? What am I meant to do with my own life? What are these strange intimations that I feel from time to time that I am meant for something bigger and greater?'

Ah, the thoughts may come but they dismiss them. They have never faced them. They do not understand themselves; they do not understand life and its meaning and its purpose. They are just the victims of what may happen to them. If a bit of good fortune comes they are happy, if it is bad they become miserable and disconsolate. Their lives are at the mercy of other people and what other people may do or say or think; they are not in control; they do not know where they are; nothing is mapped out.

And that leads to my next point which is that they have no sense of direction. There is no goal. Not having any roads in their lives, they cannot say, 'I'm going to set out from here in order to arrive there,' because there is no road. They have no objective in life at all; they have nothing to look forward to. Have you noticed sometimes when you have read the biographies of men and women who are not Christians how prominently this comes out?

I must confess it always saddens me. When I read of people who have been great, if you like, as politicians or singers or artists or something like that, and then at last they have reached an age when they can no longer carry on. They have lost their voice perhaps, or they have become too old to get new ideas, and they sit down and write their autobiography. And what is it? Well, it is all looking back. They never look forward, and you somehow feel it as you go on reading the book. You say, 'How many more years have they got left? They are coming to the end of their careers and what then?'

Well, there is nothing. They recall the moments of their triumphs, the times they made their great achievements, and it is very thrilling, it is very wonderful. But there is nothing to look forward to. It just seems to have come and gone. There was not a steady purpose, there was no goal, and at the end they are left with nothing, just emptiness. The road seems to have gone so far, then there is a sudden end, as it were. There is no direction.

But above all—and this, perhaps, is one of the saddest things about this trackless, pathless kind of heart and life—when they find themselves in a crisis or an emergency, there is nowhere they can go for help and sustenance. There they are, living this kind of heedless, thoughtless, unplanned life without any direction or purpose, without ever having taken true thought but just taking things as they come, and at last they find themselves in a great emergency. Something has gone terribly wrong, illness perhaps, or that of a dear one; some loss, financial or otherwise, but there is some calamity and they are in a real crisis. And there is nowhere they can go because there is no road. They may have heard that there is some 'Great Power' that can help over there; but how to get there? It will take so long to go through the brushwood, to penetrate the trackless waste and they may never arrive. They have never planned it out so they are left to themselves. It all comes down upon them and there is nowhere they can go.

Now, am I exaggerating? Again, am I being unfair when I suggest that that is the life of the vast majority of people in this world? Are you in that very situation at the moment? Have you sat down and considered life and its meaning and its purpose? Are you in control of yourself? Do you know where you are going? Have you an object and a purpose? Have you got a great highway that you can run along in the hour of your need to that source of supply and of help, without which you are lost and completely finished?

This, alas, is the tragedy of men and women as they are as the result of sin. They do not know where they are, nor where they are going—and especially they do not know it in the hour of their greatest need, when everything seems to give way beneath them. But the glory of true religion, according to the psalmist, is that it changes all that: 'Blessed is the man whose strength is in thee, in whose heart are ways'. The highways of God! The 'made roads' that solve the problem and that transform and transfigure everything. Order! There is nothing that is more glorious and wonderful about this Christian life than just this very element.

This is the great message of the Christian faith. How are these roads made? How does it happen that people who were like a trackless wilderness suddenly become like a charted territory, with the great highways and arterial roads and branches mapped out perfectly, and with everything in order so that they know where they are and what they can do.

Well, the answer is all there in 2 Corinthians 4:6: 'God, who commanded the light to shine out of darkness, hath shined in our hearts, to give the light of the knowledge of the glory of God in the face of Jesus Christ.' Paul was thinking there of Genesis 1:1–3, the first three verses in the Bible: 'In the beginning God created the heaven and the earth. And the earth was without form, and void; and darkness was upon the face of the deep'—or chaos was upon the surface of it all. 'And the Spirit of God moved upon the face of the waters. And God said, Let there be light: and there was light.' And from that moment the chaos disappeared, order began to come in and life and creation came into being and God looked at it all and 'saw that it was good' (v 4).

That is exactly what happens in Christianity. Into the chaos and disorder and the trackless waste of a man's life comes the operation and activity of the blessed Holy Spirit of God. Oh, thank God it is still true! That is the thing which made Saul of Tarsus an apostle; that into the chaos of his life God shone in the face of Jesus Christ, as He had done over the cosmos at the beginning, and order came into the disorder that had previously been characteristic of his life. It is like a land being mapped out and planned when the Holy Spirit begins to do His blessed work.

What is this work? It is to lead us to repentance and to regeneration. Repentance is described in Isaiah 40, and the description is quoted in Matthew 3 as that which 'prepares the way of the Lord' (Is 40:3; Mt 3:3). Repentance prepares us for the reception of the Lord Jesus Christ and His new life. It is the command to 'make a highway for our God', and this is how it is done: 'Every valley shall be exalted and every mountain and hill shall be made low' and the 'rough places' shall be made smooth (Is 40:4). Have you not seen something like that being done in this country? The land is bumpy and irregular, but no one makes a road like that, as a kind of switchback! Instead you take off these mountains, as it were, and you make them into a plain so that you end up with a level highway.

The Holy Spirit does something like that. The Holy Spirit is the greatest leveller in the world—to use a modern illustration, He is a divine bulldozer. He just flattens! He convicts us of our sin; and, when we think that we are great and mighty and knowledgeable and that we can manage our own affairs, He just puts us flat on the ground and shows us that we know nothing; that 'we have all sinned and come short of the glory of God' (Rom 3:23); that our lives are as I have been describing and that we are nothing at all: 'Every high mountain shall be brought low' (Is 40:4). And then, when we are so low as to think that we can never rise and that we are hopeless and damned, He raises us up again.

'Ah,' said the ancient Simeon to Mary, the mother of the Lord Jesus Christ, as he held the infant in his arms, 'this Child is set for the fall and rising again of many in Israel' (Lk 2:34). The leveller! The new road that is made: 'Prepare ye the way of the Lord, make straight in the desert a highway for our God' (Is 40:3). Repentance!

And not only repentance, but also regeneration—the new life or faculty, the new principle of life that is put into us by the operation of the Holy Spirit. For it is not enough merely to pull down; you need some substance. You require a plan, some direction, and it all comes in Christ.

Let us also never forget that this is a work that can only be done by the Spirit of God. You see, mankind, forgetting the Holy Spirit, failing to realise that redemption is the work of God and of Him alone, has been trying to save itself. That is the meaning of planning and of philosophy, and the world has been very busy trying to clear the trackless waste, has it not? It has been doing so for centuries and we have been told that at last we have got the expert method; but where is it? Look at the chaos in the world, look at the utter confusion. Look at the nations—they know not where they are and nobody knows where we are going. What is the value of your philosophy in the modern situation? Or all your art and all that the world has produced? Is there a highway? Where is it?

No! This is a work that God—and God alone—can do: 'God who commanded the light to shine out of darkness hath shined in our hearts' and has said, 'Let there be light and let the chaos disappear and order come in' and it comes. What does it lead to? Well, He gives us a clear view of life, a new way of thinking. The

Apostle Paul, again once and for ever, has put this thing so perfectly that I simply repeat his words: 'The natural man,' he says, 'receiveth not the things of the Spirit of God: for they are foolishness unto him: neither can he because they are spiritually discerned' (1 Cor 2:14). This new man in Christ, says Paul, is a new creature, he is a 'new creation' (2 Cor 5:17). No one understands him, but he understands all things. What is his secret? It is that 'we have the mind of Christ' (1 Cor 2:16)—a new understanding.

We must never go wrong on this. Christianity is truth, and truth comes to the mind and truth is intellectual. This is not sob stuff; this is no emotionalism. The very first thing that happens to people who become Christians is that they begin to think straighter; the highway of the mind is laid open and they begin to see life as they have never seen it before. It comes and gives them a new understanding, and for the first time ever they have a whole view of life.

To put it another way, the Gospel of Jesus Christ gives men and women a clear view of themselves. They see themselves as under God and in relationship to Him, so that they begin to see it all properly. They begin to understand themselves and the causes of their failure and misery. Until then they thought that all unhappiness was because of somebody else. Other people were not behaving themselves as they should, whereas they were perfect, and if only other people would be the same. But those others were saying the same about them! So they do not understand, the whole thing is chaos and then things go wrong. 'Why should they go wrong with me, what have I done?' They do not understand.

But the moment they become Christians they begin to see it. They realise that they are as they are and that things have happened to them very largely because of their sin, because of their folly in separating themselves and cutting themselves off from the life of God; because they have made themselves autonomous beings, which they are not and never can be, but which they have persuaded themselves that they are. And there they are, alone. They have cut themselves off from the eternal blessings and all the consequences follow on from that. But they begin to see that and they begin to see that the whole world is as it is today for the same reason. Men and women are selfish and self-centred and therefore jealous and envious. As a result, they think of war and aggrandise-ment with each one wanting to be on top and hating all others who are trying to do the same thing, so that the whole world is upside down and in a state of chaos. They begin to see it all, so they are no longer bewildered as to what the matter is with themselves nor with others.

But, thank God, they go beyond that. They see how it can all be put right. They see that all self-effort will lead to nothing, that all attempts at self-reformation are a pure waste of time. They sud-denly see that into this uncharted, trackless waste, God has sent down His own Son with a plan laid out before Him. With a redemption! And He has made a way for men and women, in their chaotic condition, to God, to redemption, to order, to salvation, to blessings that can never be described adequately.

In other words, let me put it like this; all the New Testament epistles are, in a sense, just a map of life. They start off with the great doctrines, and there you are given the understanding, the insight, the intellectual apprehension. There is no more intellec-tual book in the world than the Bible, and our own intellects will never grasp it until they have been enlightened by the Spirit. It is food for the mind; something to look at for all eternity.

So, I can state confidently, and to the glory of God in Jesus Christ, 'I understand life; I understand myself.' I understand life and I am not a bit surprised that the world is as it is. I could have prophesied it. I began preaching in the 1920s when people were still optimistic. There had been one World War but they said, 'It is all right, we'll never do that again.' They were preaching with optimism and I began preaching chaos and sin and man as he is, and I prophesied that war would come. Of course I did, there was nothing clever about that, I simply believed my Bible. I simply had a view of life presented to me there plainly and clearly. While mankind is sinful there will be wars, and it is just idle fancy and nonsense to imagine that while men and women are self-centred and selfish, they will do anything but fight one another in some shape or form. James has said it all: 'From whence comes wars and fightings among you? Come they not hence, even of your lusts that war in your members?' (Jas 4:1).

No! There is no difficulty about understanding the world if you are a Christian and if you believe this message. It is all here, it is a perfect, complete view of life.

But the gospel also gives us a sense of purpose and direction. It shows us that life is, after all, just a pilgrimage and that we are only strangers and sojourners in this world. Christians start by seeing that and they are not depressed by that. On the contrary, they have a sense of direction; they are working to a goal. They see themselves as travellers. Of course, the people who are unhappy think this is the only life and the only world and, therefore, they are horrified at the thought of death, because for them going out of this world is the last calamity. They say about a person who dies, 'Poor old so-and-so.' But Christians do not; they have a purpose.

Not only that, Christians have a system of living and an order in it. The non-Christian has no system or order, no discipline. He says, 'If I want a thing, I must have it. If I like a thing, why shouldn't I have it? Somebody else wants it? What does it matter? I want it, so I'm going to have it!' Hence, so much divorce and all the rest of it.

But when people become Christians a way is made in their lives, not only an intellectual but also a moral one. Those great New Testament epistles to which I referred not only have great doctrines at the beginning, they then go on to apply them. They say, 'In the light of this road on which you are travelling, do not wander here and there, but go straight on.' We are given moral understanding, here is planning, roads are made, everything fits in together, there is a great purpose in life. 'Blessed is the man,' says the psalmist towards the end; 'no good thing will he withhold from them that walk uprightly.' And what makes people walk uprightly is the fact that they are walking along a highway. They are no longer crouching there in a trackless waste, trying to brush away all these obstructions. No, here is a road now, a highway made by God, a way of holiness. They know what they are doing; they are disciplined, they have a scheme in life. It is all there in the injunctions, in the Old Testament and in the New.

But I must add this to show you the complete contrast with the other life, and this is in many ways the most marvellous and wonderful thing of all. It is that when they meet calamity and trials, these men and women, having a highway in their lives, know where the road is, so they do not sit there frantically saying, 'If only there were a road and a way. If only I could get there but I can't, I can't get through this brushwood!' The road is wide open.

> When all things seem against me;
> To drive me to despair,
> I know one gate is open,
> One ear will hear my prayer.
>
> Oswald Allen

The highway to God! It is already there, it has already been put within them. Christ has implanted it through the Spirit and they can go straight onto it.

But, finally, let me put that in terms of the second picture which the psalmist uses. 'Blessed,' he says, 'is the man whose strength is in thee, in whose heart are ways. Who passing through the valley of Baca make it a well.' The Christian life not only brings order into my life but because it does so it enables me to rejoice even in the midst of tribulations. The 'valley of Baca' is described in another translation like this: 'As they go through the vale of tears, they make it a place of springs.' The 'valley of Baca', therefore, is better translated as the valley of tears; the valley of sighing or of sorrow. Some say that Baca stands for some particular kind of tree called a tear tree, while others say that the word 'Baca' itself should really be translated tears, but it does not matter; the idea is the same in both. It is a place of weeping.

You notice, also, that he says it is a valley. Now a valley, in Scripture, always carries the idea of being down in the depths. When we are in a place that is shut in and hemmed in, and when there are trials and tribulations, and everything is calculated to make us miserable and utterly dejected and disconsolate—the valley of Baca—it is then that the psalmist says of God's people, 'who [while] passing through the valley of Baca make it a well.'

They turn it into 'a place of springs'. They are in a place that tends to unloose the springs of our tears and the fountains of our eyes. 'Ah yes,' he says, 'but these men and women have got something within them that enables them to turn that valley into a place of joyful springs of delight and of glory and of happiness. They make it, even while they are in it, "a place of springs".'

Now, this is astounding! This man does not hesitate to say that, and you will find as you read the psalms that they are always making this claim. Furthermore, thank God, this is something to which the saints of the centuries have always testified. They have said that the blessings of this Christian life are always great and glorious and wonderful but, that they are greatest of all in times of trouble. Read the lives of some of them—even those in our own life time in the concentration camps in Germany and in other places—and you will find that they all say this; they say with the author of the 119th Psalm, 'It is good for me that I have been afflicted' (v 71). 'Yes,' they say, 'it's in the furnace that you find the value of the Gospel. It is there!'

Now this is the test of any view of life, is it not? It is all very well to have a cheerful view of life while the sun is shining and when you are on your holidays. Here is the test: what are you like when everything goes wrong? When everything turns against you and all your world and all your dreams and hopes seem to come crashing to the ground at your feet? 'In the valley of Baca', in the place of weeping where trial comes upon trial and tribulation upon tribulation. What are you like there? That is the test!

These men and women, according to the psalmist, triumph even in the valley of Baca. It means that they are no longer victims of their circumstances. There are those who were the nicest people in the town when everything was going well and they had plenty of money in their pockets. They were the happiest people in the world and they thought that religion was very morbid and very depressing. But suddenly they have lost their health, or their work, or their money. They have lost their friends and they are down and out, disconsolate and miserable. They cannot be roused, they cannot be cheered; they are entirely defeated. The valley of Baca gets them down and they can do nothing. They can try with a kind of stoical fortitude not to whimper and cry but they have no consolation. They do not know what to do.

But not so these other men and women! No, when they pass through the valley of Baca, they make it a well. They turn weeping into a spring. You see, they do not just put up with it; they do not just manage to go through with it, they are 'more than conquerors' (Rom 8:37). Read again what David says in Psalm 23: 'Yea, though I walk through the valley of the shadow of death, I will fear no evil; for thou art with me, thy rod and thy staff they comfort me' (v 4). Even in that valley there is something that fills him with joy and happiness. Then listen to the Apostle Paul saying it gloriously in Philippians 4: 'I know both how to be abased and how to abound.... I can do all things through Christ which strengtheneth me' (vs 12–13). 'I do not care where I am,' says Paul, in effect. 'I do not care what happens to me; I do not care what is going on around me—I am what I am in Christ and I triumph in Him!' 'Rejoice in the Lord alway,' he says, 'and again I say rejoice!' (Phil 4:4). Even in the valley of Baca! We not only 'rejoice in hope of the glory of God', says Paul in the Epistle to the Romans (Rom 5:2), but more than that, 'we glory in tribulations also' (Rom 5:3).

What is the secret? Oh, I have already been giving the answer. It is their view of life that enables them to do that, it is the fact that they have got these 'ways'. You see, it works like this. What is the effect of troubles in the valley of Baca upon them? Just this: the troubles make them think all the more about God and about Christ. When they were not in the valley, there were many other things to do, but suddenly all has gone and they are left alone, and that in itself makes them go back to God; and to go back to God is to rejoice and to think of Christ and what He has done for them and their rejoicing is increased.

This is the whole secret of the Christian life. The more things go against us the more they drive us to Christ, and the more we are with Christ the happier we are. So we turn our valleys of Baca into wells and into places of rejoicing.

And, in addition, here I am a pilgrim, going through this world. I know that I must start with that, with the fact of death, the fact that I am going to die and I do not know when. I am not afraid of that, I have put it down on my map. There is the road and I am going along it. Very well, I thank God for all the light the gospel has given me, but suddenly I find myself in a valley of Baca. I am not promised that I shall not be sent there. Christ said, 'In the world you shall have tribulations but be of good cheer; I have overcome the world' (Jn 16:33).

Yes, Christians do find themselves in the valley of Baca sometimes, but, you see, they turn that into a spring, a place of wells and of rejoicing. And they do it in this way. They say, 'Yes, I am here now, but our light affliction which is but for a moment worketh for us a far more exceeding and eternal weight of glory' (2 Cor 4:17). 'Ah,' says the Christian, 'I am in the valley of Baca, my health is going, my powers are waning, my loved ones are taken from me. I know! Why should I ever have thought that that would not happen to me? Of course it must happen, but it is all right—this life is a temporary journey, I am only here as a sojourner, I am going on. I am a child of God, I am a pilgrim of eternity. I know that a glory awaits me there that baffles description.' Christians are able to say something like this:

> When all created streams are dry,
> thy fulness is the same.

Whatever may be true of the valley of Baca, God never changes. And so they can go on and add this:

> The storm may roar without me,
> My heart may low be laid;
> But God is round about me,
> And can I be dismayed?
>
> Green pastures are before me,
> Which yet I have not seen;
> Bright skies will soon be o'er me,
> Where the dark clouds have been.
> My hope I cannot measure:
> My path to life is free:

My Saviour has my treasure,
And He will walk with me.

Anna Laetitia Waring (1820–1920), 'In heavenly love
abiding'.

My beloved friends, are there 'ways' in your life? Is the highway of God and of Christ in you? Do you know where you are in this world? Do you know where you are going? Have you understanding? Is it all clear to you? Face it honestly, and if you have to admit it scares you, go and admit it to God. Plead with Him, ask Him to do the mighty operation of the Holy Spirit, to send the bulldozer and to clear the waste and to make His own way in your soul that will bring you to Himself.

And once you know Him and once you know Christ and that you are safe in Him, whatever valley of Baca you may chance to have to go through, you, as certainly as this psalmist of old, will make it a well. Oh, the blindness of men and women in sin that do not recognise such riches, such glory, such an amazing offer! But here it is: 'Blessed is the man that trusteth in thee.' Oh yes, thrice blessed! There is no happiness comparable to this: understanding, order, discipline and a blessed hope that will 'never fade away' (1 Pet 1:4). Amen.

5 LIMITING GOD

Yea, they turned back and tempted God,
and limited the Holy One of Israel
(PS 78:41).

I WANT PARTICULARLY TO DEAL with that last phrase: 'limited the Holy One of Israel'. In this psalm, the psalmist is reviewing the long history of the children of Israel. His object in doing so is to remind his own generation, and those that were to come, of the peculiar relationship of these people to God. But in this review he comes across many things that are sad and discouraging and that are so terribly wrong. Here were men and women who were the people of God, brought into being in a miraculous manner by God calling Abraham, turning him into a nation and giving them very special promises. They were His own particular possession, a people whom He had thus made for Himself in order that through them, and by means of them, He might manifest Himself finally to the whole world and reveal His great glory.

The object and function of these people, therefore, was to show forth God's praises. And yet, as the psalmist reminds them, and reminds us also, in making this review of their past history, they cut a very sorry figure. They are to be found grumbling, rebelling, complaining, defeated by their enemies, in a condition sometimes even of utter disgrace. So what the psalmist does is to give a catalogue of these various happenings in the history of the children of Israel, and as he does so he gives the reason and the explanation of it all. And his object, of course, is to show why it was that these people, who were meant for such different things, were ever to be found in this miserable, unhappy and defeated state.

But my concern here is to focus on the particular reason that he gives in the second half of verse 41, because here, it seems to me, is the most serious thing of all, the thing which above everything else is most regrettable in this long and chequered history of these people. The ultimate charge which he brings against them is that they were guilty of 'limiting the Holy One of Israel'. Now some translations translate this as 'they provoked the Holy One of Israel', which comes to the same thing. They provoked Him in this way: in their unbelief and in their failure to receive His promises and to believe them and to act upon them, they stood between themselves and the many blessings which God had offered them and promised them so freely.

Now, that is the essence of the charge which the psalmist brings against these people. It is a very common charge in the Scriptures. In other words, the children of Israel, by their unbelief, because of their state and condition, had not been living as God intended them to live; they had not risen to the heights of their high calling. Rather they were living in a state of misery and weakness and sometimes utter dejection, when they were meant to stand out as the people of God reflecting His everlasting and eternal glory. We see the same theme in Psalm 81, where God speaks of what might have been true of them if only they had hearkened to Him and walked in His way. In verse 11 He says:

But my people would not hearken to my voice;
and Israel would have none of me.
So I gave them up unto their own heart's lust;
and they walked in their own counsels.

Then He goes on:

Oh that my people had hearkened unto me,
and Israel had walked in my ways!

I should soon have subdued their enemies,
and turned my hand against their adversaries.
The haters of the Lord should have submitted themselves
unto him: but their time should have endured forever.
He should have fed them also with the finest of the
wheat: and with honey out of the rock,
should I have satisfied thee.

This is how it might have been, but it was not like that, and everywhere in the Old Testament Scriptures, in these various summaries and in particular in these psalms, we see that in various ways, God's people had been guilty of 'limiting the Holy One of Israel'.

And so, as far as we are concerned, it seems to me that we can do nothing better than examine ourselves in the light of this statement. For we, as Christian people, are the children of God. The very terms which are applied to them in the Old Testament are applied to us in the New. The Apostle Peter, quoting what God said to the children of Israel just before the giving of the Law on Mount Sinai, puts it like this: 'Ye are a chosen generation, a royal priesthood, an holy nation, a peculiar people; that ye should show forth the praises of him who hath called you out of darkness into his marvellous light' (1 Pet 2:9).

That is our position. That is our calling as Christians. We are God's people and we are meant to show forth His praises, His excellences, His virtues. So, therefore, the question that we must ask ourselves is are we doing that? Are we individually enjoying the blessings of the Christian life as we should? What do we find as we look back and review the past year? We have attended the house of God, we have read the Scriptures, but how much of this have we appropriated? To what extent are we *enjoying* all that God has offered us so freely? Are we enjoying this finest of the wheat, the honey out of the rock? What is the state and condition of our spiritual experience at this very moment? And what is the position of the whole Christian church as she finds herself in this difficult world at this troubled time? How is the church really standing out and functioning? Is she as 'an army with banners'? Is she filled with the glory of God? Is she really showing forth His excellences, the praises of Him who has called us out of darkness into His most marvellous light?

Let me put it like this: are we guilty in some shape or form of 'limiting the Holy One of Israel'? Now, this is a very striking phrase. God is almighty and omnipotent, He is a sovereign Lord, and yet the teaching is quite plain here as it is everywhere in the Bible, namely that it is possible for us, in this respect, to 'limit the Holy One of Israel' and to cause God to say, 'O that my people had hearkened unto me, O that they had listened.'

This is a paradox of course, a final antinomy that we cannot resolve. It is the same sort of thing as we find our Lord doing just before His death as He looks at Jerusalem and says, 'O Jerusalem, Jerusalem, how oft....' He would have guarded them and protected them as a hen her chickens, but they would not. It is the same idea, this charge that is constantly brought. Now, it is not for us to understand the final antinomy, but it is for us to accept the plain teaching of the Scripture. We know that ultimately God's purposes are sure and will be brought to pass, but it is equally clear that we can rob ourselves of many of God's rich blessings. We can enter into this state and condition which was so true of the children of Israel and thereby be guilty of limiting God.

It is, therefore, an urgent matter for us from the standpoint of our own personal happiness and enjoyment of the Christian life to make sure that we are not guilty of this, but, beyond that, there is this tremendous responsibility that comes upon the Christian church as a whole at this present time. With the world as it is, in its utter hopelessness and despair, have we something to offer it? Are we giving the impression that with God all things are possible? Or are we somehow or another limiting Him?

Let us try to examine ourselves in the light of this. I can only put some general questions here, trusting that the Holy Spirit will enable us to apply them to ourselves one by one. First of all: what is the standard? How are we to judge ourselves? Obviously, we cannot do so without a yardstick, some means of evaluating ourselves, and we have this, of course, quite clearly in the Bible. This is the way for us to examine ourselves. What is possible to us?

What is held out before us in the Scriptures? We read here of 'exceeding great and precious promises'. We are told that they are given to us, that all things that pertain to life and godliness are bestowed on us freely, here in the word of God. So, the question arises, to what extent are we experiencing them in our daily lives?

Then, of course, in addition to that, we have the further standard provided by the history of the church. We can read of those who have gone before us. We can read of times when the Christian church has been thrilling with power and has been a might in the land. That is another way whereby we can test ourselves. We can take up Christian biographies; we can read the lives of saints in all ages and see what is possible to a human being in this life and in this world.

Those, then, are two of the means by which we can examine ourselves, and we are exhorted to do so. 'Examine your own selves,' says the Apostle Paul to the Corinthians. 'Prove your own selves whether ye be in the faith' (2 Cor 13:5). And as the psalmist does here, it is a good thing to look back and examine ourselves in the light of these things.

Let me suggest to you some particular ways in which we can apply to ourselves the standards and the tests which we find here. Nobody can read the New Testament without seeing there a very clear picture of the Christian and of what is possible to Christian men and women. You find it, of course, in our Lord's own teaching in the Sermon on the Mount for example, and it is elaborated very clearly and plainly in the various New Testament Epistles. They are all concerned to hold up before those early Christians the pattern, the standard, the norm for Christian people and for Christian living. They are always reminding them of what is possible to them.

Now, this reminder became necessary because of failure, because people were already slipping, falling below what they were meant to be. So the New Testament authors wrote their epistles—they could not always visit the churches, so they sent them letters instead. And what they did every time was to remind the Christians of who and what they were. You always start, therefore, with doctrine. 'Here it is,' the writers say in effect, 'this is what is possible.' Then the people are examined in the light of that; they are upbraided and reprimanded and then exhorted to conform to the pattern. 'Put off...the old man...put on the new man' (Eph 4:22–24). 'You must not go on doing that,' Paul says, 'because you are no longer in that position. You have been moved. Very well, you ought to be living like this.'

The whole time, therefore, these writers are presenting their readers with this standard, and as we all examine ourselves in the light of this, we should ask ourselves whether we are conforming to the pattern, or whether we are, in some way or another limiting the Holy One of Israel. We know what God has done; we know that He has sent His only begotten Son into the world. What for? That He might form a people for Himself. You see, He has done now, in a much bigger way, what He had done of old through Abraham. Christ has been sent into the world that He might be 'the first-born among many brethren', the new humanity, and we are told what is possible to such people. And if we are not aware of it, if we are not experiencing it, we are guilty in various ways of limiting God.

So let me put before you some of the things that ought to be true of us as Christians. First, there is *assurance of salvation*, knowing that our sins are forgiven; the ability to say, 'Being justified by faith we have peace with God' (Rom 5:1) and 'there is therefore now no condemnation to them that are in Christ Jesus' (Rom 8:1). Now, that is meant to be the normal experience for every Christian. The Christian should know that his sins or her sins are forgiven. We should not be in trouble about that, or hesitating, or uncertain, or unhappy about it. We are offered here a full assurance; it is in almost every one of the New Testament Epistles. Listen to the Apostle John: 'These things I have written unto you, that ye might know that ye have eternal life' (1 Jn 5:13); 'if any man sin we have an advocate with the Father, Jesus Christ the righteous' (1 Jn 2:1); 'if we confess our sins, he is faithful and just to forgive us our sins, and to cleanse us from all unrighteousness' (1 Jn 1:9).

However, if we are uncertain about our forgiveness, we are definitely limiting God, and we have no right to be like that. God is our Father and a father never wants his children to be unhappy, to be uncertain about the relationship—the thing is inconceivable. So, we have this abundant teaching which is in the Bible to give us certainty and assurance. And if we have not got it, then we are guilty of putting a limit upon what is possible.

Yet there are many people of whom that is true. 'Oh,' they say, 'it is presumptuous to say that you know that you are forgiven;' indeed, they are actively opposed to it. But that is nothing but a 'limiting of the Holy One of Israel'. God has meant His children to know this; to know furthermore that they are His children and to know something of His love towards them.

Let me quote some scriptures to illustrate this. Take the Apostle Paul writing in Romans 5 on assurance. He says, 'We glory in tribulation also.' Why? 'Because the love of God is shed abroad in our hearts by the Holy Ghost which is given unto us' (Rom 5:3–5). He means by this that God's love is shed abroad in our hearts. He is not referring to our love for God, but to our knowledge of His love to us; that it is *shed abroad* in our hearts. And the terms are quite right because the word means shed abroad with great profusion, not just a trickle but a great outpouring of the love of God. Or take another phrase, in Romans 8:16—'The Spirit itself beareth witness with our spirits, that we are the children of God.'

Now, there is nothing beyond this. As Paul puts it in Romans 8:15—'Ye have not received the spirit of bondage again to fear; but ye have received the spirit of adoption, whereby we cry, Abba, Father.' And the Apostle is not saying that this is just something for a few chosen, special Christian people. No, he is writing to all the members of the church at Rome and this is what he assumes to be true of each and every one of them.

So the question I am asking is: are we aware of this? Are we enjoying it? Is this a description of our experience? This is how God intends us to be. The Holy Spirit was shed forth on the day of Pentecost in order to make this possible. The love of God is shed abroad in the hearts of His people to the end that they might know God's love to them and that the Spirit's witness might be authenticating it to them individually. This is not something that they deduce from the Scriptures, this is a direct witness of the Spirit, something that is made real in an immediate and direct manner to the children of God.

So I am simply arguing that if we do not know this, we are, somehow or other, guilty of 'limiting the Holy One of Israel'. Christians who merely go on hoping, wondering whether they are forgiven, whether they will ever know it, and trusting that somehow...; well, they are living as the children of Israel were living. But we are not meant to be living like that. The children of God are meant to know this love and to have an absolute assurance, an absolute certainty that their sins are forgiven and that they are, in truth and in fact, the children of God and therefore heirs of God and 'joint heirs with Christ'.

Or let me put it like this: Christian people have, of course, as the result of all this, an immediate and a direct knowledge of God and of the Lord Jesus Christ. We find some very wonderful promises about this in the Bible. The Lord Jesus, just before the end— the account is found in John 14—turns to the disciples who are so unhappy because He has announced His departure, and He says, 'Let not your heart be troubled: ye believe in God, believe also in me' (v 1). He says that He is not going to leave them comfortless; He is going to send the Holy Spirit to them, but He goes beyond that and says, 'I will manifest myself to him' (v 21).

Now, that is a very distinct and explicit promise. He says that to the one who keeps His commandments, the one who is truly Christian, He will manifest Himself, not physically, but in this spiritual manner; it is connected with the sending and the coming of the Holy Spirit. He promises to give manifestations of Himself to His people so that they shall know Him; though He is no longer with them in the flesh, He will be as real to them as He was before. That is why He also says, 'It is expedient for you that I go away: for if I go not away, the Comforter will not come unto you; but if I depart, I will send him unto you' (Jn 16:7). Why is it 'expedient'? Well, the answer is that with the indwelling of the Holy Spirit He will be present, and, in addition to that, He will give manifestations of Himself to His people. Do we know Him like that? Do we know God in a living and in a real manner?

When you read about these people in the Bible, you find that they knew God. They did not just believe things about God at a distance, He was real to them. Even the psalmist, in the Old Testament dispensation which is inferior to our position, says, 'When my father and my mother forsake me, then the Lord will take me up' (Ps 27:10). We read in Psalm 84 of the psalmist's longing for God's courts; and why? It is because there he sees God's grace and glory. Abraham was the friend of God, and we are all children of Abraham by faith; so the question is, do we know God the Father and God the Son in this intimate manner? Are we aware of these manifestations? Have we really known the presence of the living God? We are meant to. It is offered us, quite plainly in the Bible, and not only here. It is also confirmed so abundantly in the subsequent history of God's people.

An old Puritan, for example, said just before his death, 'God dealeth familiarly with men.' Why did he say that? He said it on the basis of an experience he had had of God's nearness; God had manifested something of His glory to this man. You see, these accounts in the Scriptures of people having visions of the glory of God are not imagination, they are facts, these things happen. And so you find them in the Old and the New Testament and in church history; 'God dealeth familiarly with men'.

Do you know God? Do you know anything of this familiar trafficking with Him, this communion with Him, which is real? I am not talking about just getting on your knees and saying your prayers; I am speaking about a realisation of the presence of God, God the Father and God the Son and God the Holy Spirit. We are meant to enjoy that; these are some of the exceeding great and precious promises that God has held out before us, and my argument is that if we know nothing about this, then we are guilty of limiting Him. We are not enjoying to the full what He has put at our disposal, what He has prepared for us as His people.

So the first thing that must be true of us is assurance of salvation, but that leads to the second which is *rejoicing*. God's people are meant to be a rejoicing people; these are the words of Scripture: 'Rejoice evermore' (1 Thess 5:16). Or as Paul puts it to the Philippians: 'Rejoice in the Lord alway: and again, I say, rejoice' (Phil 4:4). 'But is that possible?' you say. It is! As we have just seen, Paul also says that we even rejoice also in tribulation—in the midst of it, whatever is going wrong.

Let me give you another quotation, from the Apostle Peter this time: 'Whom [that is, the Lord Jesus Christ] having not seen; ye love; in whom, though now ye see him not, yet believing, ye rejoice with joy unspeakable and full of glory' (1 Pet 1:8). To whom was he writing? Well, when you read that first Epistle of Peter, you will find that he was not writing a circular letter to his fellow apostles. No, he was writing to the strangers scattered abroad throughout Pontus, Galatia, Bithynia, Cappadocia and various other places; people whom he had never met. But though he did not know them, he was writing to them because he had been told that they were Christian people; they were passing through a period of tribulation and so he wrote to encourage them and to help them. They were so-called ordinary Christians, just average church members, and because they were that Peter did not hesitate to say that about them; they knew what it was to 'rejoice with a joy unspeakable and full of glory'. It is a glorious rejoicing which baffles words; it is so marvellous that it is beyond any true expression.

So that is how we are meant to be as God's people. Christian people were never meant to be miserable or unhappy, and if you and I are, as it were, half turning back to the world still; rather bemoaning the fact that we cannot enjoy what the people of the world are enjoying and that we cannot still be with them; if we are thinking that we are very wonderful in denying ourselves and taking up this cross and having this hard and difficult life, oh then we are in a terrible state. It means that we are proclaiming to the world that God's way of living is a miserable one; that for true happiness and joy you go to the world and that you cannot get it here. That is 'limiting the Holy One'—the very thing that the people of Israel were guilty of. There they were—miserable, when God had held out such glorious possibilities before them. They limited Him in the matter of rejoicing.

The third thing which must be true of us as Christians is: *delighting in God and in His commandments*. The Apostle John says in his first Epistle, 'His commandments are not grievous' (1 Jn 5:3).

How can God's commandments be grievous to anybody who really has an enlightened mind? There is no life like it; this is the only life—the other is darkness. Is it possible that to a child of God the commandments should be grievous, a heavy burden to be borne? But the children of Israel were always giving that impression. They said, 'Look at those other nations; they've got kings and we haven't got one. Give us a king.' You see, they despised the fact that God was their King. They envied these other nations; those people could do what they liked. They had not got ten commandments; they did not have to observe the Sabbath; they could eat anything they liked and marry anybody they liked. 'Here are we,' said God's people, 'living this narrow life.' They were always grumbling and complaining; that was the charge brought against them.

Is that true of us? Do we find the commandments of God grievous? Do we find the way that God has mapped out for us hard and difficult and narrow and trying? Is our Christianity against the grain? Do we give the impression that it is a matter of duty or perhaps more a matter of fear than anything else? If so, my friends, we are 'limiting the Holy One of Israel'. He meant us to enjoy keeping His commandments. It was meant to be our chief delight. The psalmist can say, 'Oh how love I thy Law,' and we are in a superior position to the psalmist; we have a fulness that he did not know.

Surely these things are plain and clear, but let me go on. Are we enjoying *the peace of God?* We are meant to. Let me remind you of more of Paul's words in Philippians 4: 'Be careful for nothing; [In nothing be anxious] but in every thing by prayer and supplication with thanksgiving let your requests be made known unto God. And the peace of God which passeth all understanding shall keep your hearts and minds through Christ Jesus' (vs 6–7).

These are practical matters. Have you enjoyed that peace during the last year? Different things have happened to us all: trials, tribulations, sorrow, perhaps loss. I do not know what it is, but I do know that the Apostle said, 'In every thing,' and that is all inclusive, there is no exception. So have you experienced it? Or when the trials have come, have you been utterly distracted and distraught, have you been beside yourself, have you been confused, alarmed? Have you felt like grumbling and complaining, 'Why is God doing this to me?' Which has it been? The children of Israel were always unhappy and restless, not knowing the peace, and it was because they were 'limiting the Holy One of Israel'. They did not know His comfort; they would not let Him give it. They turned away from Him instead of turning to Him. How has it been with us? There is no question about this; if we are not knowing something of 'the peace of God that passeth all understanding' to that extent, we are limiting God.

But if we are really in this true relationship to God then, whatever may happen, we can know this peace that nothing can disturb; it is our duty to enjoy it and we are sinning if we do not. It is as possible to us as it was to the Apostle Paul, and we should know it; we should know as a reality and experience that 'all things work together for good to them that love God, to them who are the called according to his purpose' (Rom 8:28). Not to know it is to put a limit on what God has made possible for us.

Another mark of the true Christian is: *resting in Him and in His all-sufficiency*. We find that, too, in Philippians 4: 'I have learned, in whatsoever state I am, therewith to be content. I know both how to be abased and I know how to abound:...I can do all things through Christ which strengtheneth me' (vs 11–13). Is that our experience? Do we know Christ to be all-sufficient? Have we found Him to be such in times of trouble and problems? Have we found Him to be everything to us? Could we sing from the heart, that wonderful hymn of Charles Wesley:

> Thou hidden source of calm repose,
>   Thou all-sufficient love divine,
> My help and refuge from my foes,
>   Secure I am, if Thou art mine:
> And lo! From sin, and grief, and shame
> I hide me, Jesus, in Thy name.
>
> Thy mighty name salvation is,
>   And keeps my happy soul above:

> Comfort it brings, and power, and peace,
>   And joy and everlasting love:
> To me, with Thy dear name, are given
> Pardon, and holiness, and heaven.

Is it true of us?

> Jesus, my all in all thou art;
>   My rest in toil, my ease in pain.

Is He? Is He that to you?

> The medicine of my broken heart,
>   In war my peace, in loss my gain,
> My smile beneath the tyrant's frown,
> In shame my glory and my crown:

> In want my plentiful supply,
>   In weakness my almighty power,
> In bonds my perfect liberty,
>   My light in Satan's darkest hour,
> My help and stay whene'er I call,
> My life in death, my heaven, my all.

Now, Charles Wesley, there, was writing his experience. You see, it is not only the Apostle Paul who can say, 'I can do all things through Christ which strengtheneth me.' Charles Wesley is repeating it and there are others who have said exactly the same thing.

> Thou, O Christ, art all I want,
>   More than all in Thee I find,

said Wesley in another hymn. Is it true? Yes. He is that, He is the all-sufficient one. Have we found Him to be such? If not we are limiting His power, we are limiting what is possible to the believer in this life. This is how we are meant to live. This should be our constant experience. Not to know it is, in some sense, to limit His grace and His glory.

There, then, are some of the tests which we must apply to ourselves and to the church as a whole. Read the accounts of the early church which was filled with the power of the Spirit; great grace was upon them all; the presence of the Spirit was there in power; they were conscious of it and the place where they met together was shaken. What does the church today know about all that? Here are the questions which we must ask ourselves. You read of the past and you read a man like Whitefield saying, 'Christ came down amongst us.' Do we know anything about that? Do we ever expect Him to come down? We read of men talking about 'days of heaven upon earth', do we know anything like that? Do we know what it is to God in the midst, and the presence of the Holy Spirit thrilling the whole congregation with His power and His grace and His glory? These are the things that are offered, the things that are made possible by all that the Son of God did when He came here upon earth.

Those, then, are some of the questions we must ask ourselves, and if we find that we are guilty of limiting God, let me give you some of the causes. I find them in this psalm and I add a few to them. The first and most common cause of all, of course, is *sin and disobedience*. It was because this was constantly true of them that the children of Israel were brought to calamity and made miserable and wretched. And you, too, will never know the blessings of this Christian life until you stop sinning, and until you begin to obey God's commandments. It follows as the night the day; it is no use asking for blessings if you are deliberately continuing in sin. That is the most common cause of all.

Let me add a second: *self-satisfaction*—self-confidence and self-reliance. That, again, was a constant source of trouble in the children of Israel. They did not need the power of God; they could gather an army; they could muster their forces; they could have good generals of their own! They did not need God, so they went and challenged the enemy in their own strength and were always defeated. But when they trusted in God, even though they were only a handful, they were always victorious. Self-confidence, self-satisfaction, this feeling that we have arrived!

I read many religious periodicals today and I could come to the conclusion from them that things have never been going so well. Everything is all right! That is the impression they give—with the church in utter weakness and more or less paralysed. It is tragic, this self-confidence that still continues; this belief that man can still organise the Christian church and be successful; this fatal self-satisfaction. People feel they have become Christians, so what more is necessary? Everything is all right, and the moment you begin to feel that, you have shut off the blessings of God. He only blesses the humble and those who are truly contrite.

Another cause of trouble is *ignorance and blindness*. 'What do you mean by that?' asks someone. I mean ignorance of what is taught in the Scriptures. There are so many people who never seem to have realised what is possible to a Christian. They think that to be a Christian means that you just make your decision; you take a certain step and that is all. They know nothing about the things I have been holding before you; they never seem to have read of them or to be aware of them. But here they are in the Scriptures. And it is not only ignorance of the Bible, it is also ignorance of history. That was the trouble with these children of Israel. Notice the eleventh verse: 'They forgat His works, and His wonders that He had shewed them.' They were always forgetting it. A generation arose that 'knew not Joseph'; a generation came that did not know the wonderful things that God had done as He brought the people of Israel out of Egypt into Canaan; they were ignorant of the history of their own past. That is why the psalmist reminds them of it. And there are so many today who know nothing about periods of awakening and of revival and of God coming down; they know nothing of what is possible to individuals; and all through sheer ignorance of the facts of the history of the Christian church.

Then, of course, there is always *unbelief*—not taking the Bible as it is. Or if they do read it, people explain it away in terms of their own experience—'limiting the Holy One of Israel'. 'But,' they say, 'you're misinterpreting that. When it talks about the

Holy Ghost or the love of God being "shed abroad in our hearts", that is true of all Christians. It isn't a matter of experience, it's a matter of a statement. If the Holy Spirit is in you, then that is true.' Is it? Now that is to limit God, to reduce the promises to the level of our experience, indeed to our poverty of experience.

Or perhaps we may not believe that it is possible for us. So many are in that position. They read the New Testament and they say, 'Yes, that's all right; those were the early days. Those were the apostles, we are not all meant to be like that.' Who told you so? The Scripture says, 'The promise is unto you, and to your children, and to all that are afar off' (Acts 2:39). There is no limit! Nowhere does the New Testament say that this life is only possible to the first generation of Christians. It is meant to be for all, all Christians at all times and in all places, and if you are guilty of that misinterpretation, you are guilty of 'limiting the Holy One of Israel'.

Finally, there is *wrong belief*. That is partly what we have been considering already, that this life is only meant for certain special people. That is the heresy of dividing Christians up into those who are saints and those who are not; but according to the New Testament, we are all called to be saints. So we must not excuse ourselves by saying, 'But I'm not one of these special people.' We are all special people and we are all the children of God.

And then there is a very terrible wrong belief which is a kind of fatalism, very often a misunderstanding of the teaching of the sovereignty of God, a belief which says, 'Oh, this is a time of declension. This is not a time to expect blessing either individually or for the church, so don't ask for it. You must just wait until times will improve.' But that is a blank contradiction of the teaching of these psalmists. At such times the psalmists pleaded with God to come back. They said, 'Why are you as a journeyman, or as a stranger; why don't you come back?' And that is the inevitable attitude of a child. But the other view is sheer fatalism and has nothing to do with the teaching of Scripture.

Another belief that is very common today is the tendency to dismiss these high experiences as just ecstasy. People try to explain them psychologically as the enthusiasm of youth, or people being carried away, or emotionalism. But that is to 'limit the Holy One of Israel'; that is to quench the Spirit. That is to put a barrier between that which God has made possible for us and ourselves. No! We are meant to enjoy these things.

The last cause of trouble, perhaps, is *fear*. Fear of the cost of these things; fear of the consequences; fear of persecution; fear of laughter; fear of mockery; fear of jeering. Fear that if you put yourself into the hands of God, you never know what He will ask you to do and therefore you hold back and 'limit the Holy One of Israel'. What a terrible thing.

Those, then, are the causes of the trouble, so what do we do about it? Well we must see the enormity of it all. Is there anything more terrible than to limit God? We must realise the harm that is done to the name of God, to His glory and kingdom, and to God's cause, that we His people should present such a picture. It is God's name that is tarnished. We have limited Him in the sight of the people. What a terrible crime! What an awful sin. The enormity of it all and the harm it does to His name!

But think of the utter folly of it from our own standpoint. Is there any person more miserable than the person who has got just enough Christianity to make him miserable and to spoil everything the world has got? Awful! But there are many like that. They have no joy of salvation; they have no joy in the Lord; they know nothing about these great blessings of the Christian life. It is all negative; they have had to give up, and there they are, as it were, naked and negative. Oh, what a tragedy!

So, to the extent that we have all felt ourselves guilty of this charge of 'limiting the Holy One of Israel', let us repent. Let us go back to God as soon as we can; let us confess and acknowledge the sin and the folly and the shame of it all, and then let us listen to what He will tell us. This is what He will tell you: 'Open thy mouth wide and I will fill it' (Ps 81:10). That is what He wants us to do, not just to open it, but to open it *wide*. Let Him fill it. Open your heart to Him, believe the promises—take them literally as they are. Do what William Carey, the real founder of missionary work, said, 'Expect great things from God. Attempt great things for God.' Listen to how another writer puts it:

Thou art coming to a King;
Large petitions with thee bring;
For His grace and power are such,
None can ever ask too much.

John Newton

Oh, open your mouths wide, open your heart to the exceeding great and precious promises. Do not give yourself any peace until you are enjoying fulness of salvation, until you are rejoicing evermore, until you know God and the Lord Jesus Christ and the Holy Spirit in a personal manner; until God's commandments are joyous to you and not grievous; and until you can say, from the very depths of your being,

Thou, O Christ, art all I want,
More than all in Thee I find.

God give us grace to do so for His glory and for the blessing and the enrichment of our own souls.   Amen.

6 *THOU ART MY GOD*

O God, thou art my God; early will I seek thee:
my soul thirsteth for thee,
my flesh longeth for thee in a dry and thirsty land,
where no water is;
To see thy power and thy glory,
so as I have seen thee in the sanctuary.
Because thy lovingkindness is better than life,
my lips shall praise thee
(PS 63:1–3).

BEFORE WE BEGIN OUR consideration of this psalm, let me remind you what a psalm is. It is a song, a kind of poem, and it therefore has a message which is complete in and of itself; so it is always essential to take a psalm as a whole. We can, of course, pause and concentrate upon particular parts, but we must always remember the whole. And it is quite obvious in the case of this psalm that there is indeed a complete message. Now this is one of these great and glorious psalms—they are all wonderful and there is a sense in which it is almost foolish to differentiate between psalm and psalm, but this one has always been a great favourite with God's people. It was used as a morning hymn by some of the early Christians and it was also the favourite hymn of one of the greatest preachers of the early centuries, John Chrysostom, the 'golden-mouthed' orator or preacher, as he was generally known. We are told also that when Theodore Beza, one of the great leaders of the Protestant Reformation, could not sleep, he would invariably recite this psalm to himself, so that though he could not sleep he was filled with a spirit of joy and of rejoicing.

It is, obviously, therefore, a psalm that speaks to God's people, and has spoken to them throughout the running centuries. Now, it is generally agreed that it was probably written by David at the time of the insurrection of his son Absalom who, for various reasons, had worked up a rebellion against his own father. David was compelled to vacate Jerusalem; he had to flee for his life; and at one point in that exodus from Jerusalem, he and his company found themselves in a wilderness. David therefore, at that moment, was a man who was full of perplexities and difficulties. People who had promised to follow him had proved treacherous to him, and his situation, in a sense, could not have been worse. As he says, 'My soul thirsteth for thee, my flesh longeth for thee in a dry and thirsty land, where no water is.' Those were the circumstances in a literal, physical sense as far as David was concerned but, of course, this was still more true in a spiritual sense.

So what we find in this psalm is an account of how David dealt with himself in that situation. Here is this man of God, hemmed in, as it were, in the wilderness, with all the trials and perplexities, and he tells us (we should thank God for this!) how he faced it all; what he did and how he reacted. He thereby teaches us, as he has taught God's people throughout the centuries, how we also should deal with ourselves when we find ourselves in a similar state and position.

Now, this is true of many individuals at the present time. There are people in trouble and trial, with grievous problems, and with everything apparently against them. And it is equally true of the Christian church as a whole. These are evil, difficult days for the Christian church. In this country we are but a little remnant in a kind of wilderness of paganism with enemies set against us, round and about us. But here, in this psalm, is a lesson as to how we should conduct ourselves at such a time and in such a situation. The method of the psalm is typical. Indeed, the chief characteristic of all the psalms—that is the wonderful thing about them—is that almost all of them are saying exactly the same thing, but they vary according to the circumstances. In other words, the presentation varies but the method is very much the same.

Let us approach it like this. A time of trouble or of difficulty is always a testing time. And what it does is to test where we really are and what we really have. So I want to approach this psalm from that particular angle because such times, above everything else, test our profession of the Christian faith. If you really want to know whether you are a Christian or not, the simplest, most direct way, always, is to discover what you are like when things go against you. A time of affluence and prosperity, when the sun is shining and everything is going well, never tests our profession. But the moment things go wrong and you are in a state of perplexity, then you will know exactly the value of what you claim to believe.

It is, alas, possible for us to have an intellectual belief in these things. The Bible contains an incomparable system of truth. Merely looked at from the standpoint of philosophy, there is nothing superior to it. It is an old book and a very wise one. It is a book that knows people; it knows life; it has an understanding; there is no profounder wisdom. And so there are many who have come to it and taken it up in that way, simply from the standpoint of its teaching and its wisdom, as something purely intellectual.

Indeed, unfortunately, it is possible for us to accept even the Christian way of salvation with our minds, in a purely theoretical, detached manner. In a sense, it is reasonable to do so—the system is such a complete one. There are people who have been brought up in the church and in the atmosphere of these things; they have received instruction and have taken it in and accepted it; indeed, there are many who say that they cannot recall a time when they did not believe it. Well, that is all right, but the real thing we need to discover is whether that is only in the mind. Is it only something theoretical? And so, let me emphasise it again, the most direct way always to discover the real value of what you claim as your profession of the Christian faith is to know how you react and how you behave in a time of trouble.

Furthermore, as well as the snare of a merely intellectual belief, there is another danger—that of depending, as it were, upon the house of God and upon its services. David puts that point here when he says, 'To see thy power and thy glory, so as I have seen thee in the sanctuary.' But now he was not in the sanctuary. He had been forced to escape from Jerusalem, and was in the wilderness. There is this constant danger: do we depend only upon the church and its services and its fellowship and all these things? For example, what are you like if you are taken ill, and are lying on your back in a bed in your home or in a hospital? You cannot go to church, nor meet with God's people and you are in difficulties. You may even be worried as to whether you are going to live or not; you do not know, the whole thing is uncertain. Or you can think of many other similar trials that may come to us; bereavement and sorrow; some loss or disappointment; the various 'slings and arrows of outrageous fortune'. These things come to us sooner or later—every one of us will eventually be in a wilderness, even if we have not been in one already; because this is a passing world and there is a final wilderness, through which we must all pass.

So here is the test: what are we like when we find ourselves in some such wilderness? Here is the supreme test of our whole profession of the Christian faith, so let us consider these tests as to whether we are truly Christian or not, as they are suggested to us by this great psalm.

The first is that like David, *the true Christian is always driven by adversity to God.* Here is David in trouble in the wilderness, and this is his reaction: 'O God, thou art my God; early will I seek thee.' This is a tremendously important point. You will find many people who have always thought that they are Christians and who have always been regarded by everybody as Christians. But when something goes wrong with them, either personally or to their loved ones, their immediate reaction is to say, 'Why has God done this to me?' They turn away from God. They become annoyed and are filled with questions, with doubts and with grumbles. They feel that God is dealing with them unfairly and unkindly. Many of them even give up their open profession, saying, 'There is nothing in it. If God is God why am I being allowed to suffer like this?' Many have left the Christian church, and have given up even any pretence of a profession of the Christian faith. Like Job's wife, they say to themselves and to one another, 'Let's curse God. What is the value of this thing if He lets us endure in this way?' And, this unfortunately, is something which is quite common.

But, the true believer does the exact opposite, and that is why this is such a subtle and thoroughgoing test. The immediate reaction of a believer in a time of trouble is to draw near to God: 'To whom shall we go but unto thee?' says the believer, in the words again of the psalmist. You will find throughout these psalms that these men, though often perplexed and in grievous positions, nevertheless always turn to Him. They are like the needle of a compass; it may flicker and vary but it always settles there on that fixed point—God. 'Early will I seek thee.'

Now, these things which we are considering together may be simple, but they are very profound, and we all know in our hearts that you cannot argue about these matters. You know immediately, there is no need of any demonstration or proof—that is the wonderful thing about life. There is a kind of instinctive reaction, and the instinctive reaction of the Christian, invariably, is to turn to God.

The second point is that *Christians not only instinctively turn to God in this way at such a time, but they feel that they have a right to do so*. They turn to God because they know Him. Christian people, when in perplexity, do not get down on their knees and pray to 'whatsoever gods may be'. That is what many do. It is a cry into empty space as it were, a cry in the void, because they do not know God. When in trouble, most people still, in spite of their godlessness and irreligion, 'offer a prayer', as they put it. But it is an act of desperation. They do not know what they are doing; they are at their wits' ends, just hoping against hope and crying out, not knowing what else they can do.

Nor does the true believer pray, as so many do, to some god who is in the distance somewhere; some remote, great, eternal being perhaps, but someone who is so far removed from this world that he does not really know or understand; a god who, in any case, cannot be interested in any particular individual and in the minutiae and details of one's personal life. So they cry out to that distant god in the vague hope that he may hear and that he may be pleased to answer. But that is not the Christian at all.

No, this is quite different. Listen to David in this psalm; here is the language always of the true children of God. He begins with an expressive exclamation: 'O God!' No one ever uses that unless he or she is a child of God. I know that the world in its blasphemy utters these two words as an expletive but it does not know what it is saying. But here the psalmist offers it from the very depth of his being: 'O God!' You sense the feeling, the whole man involved in it. He turns to the one whom he knows is going to listen. He flees to Him.

And further, you see, he is able to say, 'Thou art my God': not merely God as such but 'my God' in particular. In other words, there is a consciousness of this personal relationship. He does not go doubtfully and uncertainly; he knows that God is his God and that he is God's child. He turns as a child turns to his father with the same instinctive movement. There is no query, no doubt, no uncertainty. He knows the way is open; he has travelled so often upon it that he can at times utter nothing but his 'O!'

Let us quote the Apostle Paul on this. 'Likewise,' he says, 'the Spirit also helpeth our infirmities; for we know not what we should pray for as we ought but the Spirit itself maketh intercession for us with groanings which cannot be uttered' (Rom 8:26). And, indeed, there is all that content of meaning in this 'O' as it is uttered by the children of God. 'O God, thou art my God.' They go, therefore, into the presence of God with this certainty.

Then next, David says, 'My soul thirsteth for thee, my flesh longeth for thee in a dry and thirsty land, where no water is.' Now, I want to emphasise this because this is not expressive of a vague desire. No, it is about the profoundest feeling of which one is ever capable. So this man does not approach God in the sense that he decides on the whole, to turn to God—'let's try prayer'—having done everything else that he can. Nor does he have to persuade himself to do so. He does not have to take himself to task, as it were, and work it out and arrive at a decision. He does so, not only instinctively as we have seen, but he does so with the whole longing of his being. Of course, you find this repeatedly in the psalms: 'As the hart panteth after the water brooks'—it is the same idea—'so panteth my soul after thee, O God. My soul thirsteth for God, for the living God' (Ps 42:1). It is everywhere in the Old Testament, as it is everywhere also in the New Testament and as it is everywhere in the literature concerning God's people throughout the running centuries.

In other words, and this is the third point: *it is David's greatest desire to feel the presence of God*; to know that He is with him and that He is looking down upon him. Because David—and this is the wonderful thing—was even more concerned about this than he was about his circumstances. He is in a dry and thirsty land without water; he is surrounded by enemies; he knows that some very able men are conspiring with Absalom to bring about not only his defeat but probably his death also, in order that Absalom may become king. His situation could not be more precarious. But in spite of all this, his biggest concern is not with the circumstances, though, naturally, he is concerned about them. No, the real desire of David's heart, and he puts it therefore in this expressive language, is: 'My soul thirsteth for thee, my flesh....' The whole man is involved; there is nothing about him that is not, in this way, longing and thirsting for the presence of God.

Now, this is always a mark of the children of God. The desire for an intimate knowledge of God the Father is the biggest and the most important thing in their lives; it is of greater importance to them than anything else whatsoever and therefore they are more concerned about it; it is a deep desire to have this personal certainty.

Obviously, David, there in the wilderness, believed in God. He was not asking that his faith might be strengthened. Rather, what David wanted was to experience God in that wilderness as he had so often experienced Him in His house: 'To see thy power and thy glory, so as I have seen thee in the sanctuary.' David used to go to the sanctuary—as every godly person does, because God has promised to meet with His people. Furthermore, as David reminds us again in a very similar psalm, Psalm 84, 'grace and glory' are found in the house of God. That is why he wanted to be there; 'How amiable are thy tabernacles, O Lord of hosts!' That was the place where God had given the manifestations of Himself and had come and had met His people and where they had been thrilled together.

David had often had this personal experience of God, this

knowledge that God was directly and immediately concerned. Now, this is no mere general belief in God, this is permanent. David is here longing for just this: an assurance that God is still with him and that He will never leave him nor forsake him. He wants to have the highest experience that he has ever known in the temple. He wants that in the wilderness. And so I would emphasise both aspects of this matter. Christians, true believers, not only believe in God, they not only pray to God, this God in whom they believe: they are men and women who have experienced God; they know Him. That is what David is talking about here.

Now, this can never be emphasised too much. This is, in a sense, the difference between religion and true faith. You can take up religion, but you cannot take this up; it is something that God does to you; something which He gives you. Obviously, that is why David is seeking it, that is why he cries out for it. Indeed, this is the thing that the true child of God wants above everything else:

> Tell me Thou art mine, O Saviour;
> Grant me an assurance clear.

So says the hymn writer, William Williams. An obvious illustration from the natural realm brings this out. The one who loves always wants to know that he or she is loved in return. They do not take it for granted, they want it to be stated, and so does the child of God. Moreover, David realises, as he tells us, that this is not something that is confined to the sanctuary and this is the wonderful thing about it. 'I have known it in the sanctuary,' says David, 'but I know that it is equally possible here.' So, you see, you are not entirely dependent upon the house of God, you can experience God just as much when you are lying on a solitary bed in your home or in the hospital. When you are absolutely isolated, He can be with you there, as He can be with you in the tabernacle, in the temple, or in the church.

This was a lesson that the children of Israel were often slow to learn. Do you remember also the woman of Samaria who argued with our Lord? 'You say,' she said, in effect, 'You Jews say that one must worship in Jerusalem; we say you should worship in this mountain.' And our Lord replies, 'The hour cometh when ye shall neither in this mountain nor yet at Jerusalem worship the Father.... God is a Spirit and they that worship him must worship him in spirit and in truth' (Jn 4:21,23). The longing of the Christian is, in all circumstances and situations, just to know that God is with him and is looking upon him. It is the enjoyment of God in a personal sense, at all times and in all places: 'My soul thirsteth for thee, my flesh longeth for thee.'

Now, my friends, is this true of us? If you are not in a wilderness, is this true of you? It should be true at all times. It is true of the children of God even when everything has gone against them, but it is obviously meant to be much more true when things are going well with us and when the sun is shining down upon us. Can we say, honestly, 'My soul thirsteth for thee, my flesh longeth for thee'? Well, let me emphasise it again, if that is not your experience now, then what will you be like when you do find yourself in that wilderness?

But let us go on to the next test which is again still more thorough. David takes us a step further: 'Because thy lovingkindness is better than life, my lips shall praise thee.' Now, here is a tremendous statement. *To the true believer, God's lovingkindness is the most precious thing in life.* You cannot qualify this because David makes it as an absolute statement: 'Because thy lovingkindness is better than life.' This is really tremendous, is it not? It is, therefore, *the* test of our whole position and profession. The children of God want this presence of God, this felt realisation of God's lovingkindness; they want this above everything else.

This theme is found running right through the Bible. That was the difference, in a sense, between Abraham and Lot. Lot had his eye on the plains with its cities and its fruitfulness. But Abraham had his eye on God and was content with the mountains. Then in Philippians 1:21 there is a great statement of it by the Apostle Paul: 'For me to live is Christ.' That is life! 'That is, to me, everything in life,' says Paul, and 'to die is gain!' Or as he puts it again in Philippians 3:10, 'That I may know him; and the power of his resurrection, and the fellowship of his sufferings.' 'One thing,' says the Apostle, 'I do!' This is the whole object of his life and living: to know Him! 'Thy lovingkindness is better than life.'

Now, what David means is this—and we must not forget his circumstances, he is in this most dangerous and precarious position—what he says, in effect is, 'I'm not so much concerned about my personal safety; I'm not even ultimately concerned about going on living. I'm not just concerned about escaping from this awful predicament and the malice even of my own son who has risen against me in rebellion. Your lovingkindness is more important to me, even than life itself.'

Therefore I hold this before you again as one of these profound and fundamental tests. We are all in this uncertain world, a world that is always on the edge of some crisis, or with some final catastrophe always looming up. It may disappear temporarily, but it will come back. So here is the test: what is to us the most important thing? Is it just to go on living, to prolong life? Is death the final calamity? For many people it is, and the thing is so tragic because they have nothing but this life. Everything is in this world for them, and anything that threatens existence in this world is terrible.

But it is not so to the Christian. Nor to the true child of God: 'Thy lovingkindness is better than life.' Why? Well, I have already anticipated part of the answer, let me give you a negative first. You see, the true child of God constantly realises that this is a passing world, a transient life. Once more, this sounds so obvious and so simple, and yet I sometimes think it is the key to the whole present situation. The world today is doing its utmost to forget this profound fact: that life is transient and passing. The author of the Epistle to the Hebrews puts this in his own wonderful way: 'Here have we no continuing city, but we seek one to come' (Heb 13:14). That is the Christian: this is 'the victory that overcometh the world'. The world will always make you concentrate upon it—in its newspapers, books, journals, entertainments, in its everything. It is always fixing attention on this life, that is the whole fallacy of man in sin.

But Christians know that, so they do not put existence and continuing in this life first. That is not the chief thing with them because they know that at best it is only temporary. You are taken ill, you wonder whether you are going to get well and then you recover, thank God! And then you forget what you felt like at that awful moment. But that is where you show yourself to be a poor fool who does not know how to think. You have only had a temporary respite, because it is only a postponement. Now the Christian faces all this. That is the wisdom of the Bible: 'Here have we no continuing city.'

Christians, therefore, do not put mere perpetuation of existence in this world in the first or central place. But they have a second reason for saying this. It is that they know that life in this world can never really completely satisfy. Here again, we must examine ourselves. The child of God is someone who can say quite honestly, 'I don't know what it is, but I have never found complete satisfaction in this world as such, never. Oh, I've been interested, I've been attracted, I've been helped, I've been moved, I've had enjoyment but there is something in me, crying out for 'an ampler ether, a diviner air', some longing, some intimations, some feeling, some aspirations.'

This is partly, of course, because it is a world of trials and troubles. 'In the world,' says Christ, 'ye shall have tribulation' (Jn 16:33). The cares of this life, the things that come unexpectedly are here and you cannot avoid them. We all know this when we stop to think about it, but the devil keeps us so busy that we fail to think and when in trouble we no longer know what to do. But Christian men and women have faced it all out; and they know that life never has been able truly to satisfy them.

But, of course, they have gone even further than that. They have discovered that the world is mainly vain and empty, even at its best and highest; 'Fading is the worldling's pleasure, all its boasted pomp and show.' And Christians can see through all this; they are no longer carried away by it. There was a time when they were not Christians, and these things were everything to them but not now. They have seen that there is in all this an element of decay. It is a world where 'moth and rust doth corrupt and where thieves break through and steal' (Mt 5:19). The world at its best! 'The lust of the flesh and the lust of the eyes and the pride of life!'

(1 Jn 2:16). That is the world and Christians see through the emptiness that is involved in it all. They know that it is variable and ever-changing, and so they arrive at the same conclusion as that of the great Apostle Paul when he says, 'For we that are in this tabernacle, do groan, being burdened...earnestly desiring to be clothed upon with our house which is from heaven' (2 Cor 5:4;2).

So the true child of God has, like David, come to see that mere living, mere existence, merely going on, merely escaping your enemies, getting out of this hole or this trouble, is not the first thing. No, they have seen life steadily and seen it whole; they have seen it as it is, no longer deluded by its glamour and pretence.

That is the negative side, but oh, it is the positive that makes them speak like David. There are many people who have seen through life and who have ended in cynicism. There are many cynics in this modern world, many intelligent men and women who have enough intelligence to see the vain show, and so they retire out of it. Their attitude is: 'I cannot get excited about this, I am only fooling myself, I'm enjoying it now but when I get older I won't be able to. So what is the point of it all?' They can see through it, but they have nothing else, so they end in cynicism and in a kind of despair.

But David says, 'Thy lovingkindness is better than life.' This is not only because he knows the truth about life, but also because he knows the lovingkindness of God. It is positive. Why does David thirst for God above everything else? Why is he more concerned about this even than his circumstances and conditions? Why is he after this lovingkindness? The answer is simply because God is who and what He is: 'To see thy power and thy glory, so as I have seen thee in the sanctuary.' The glory of God, to be in the presence of God! There is nothing that is comparable to this.

It is very difficult to put this into words, so I am driven again to fall back upon the simple human analogy. If you know anything of what it means to be in love, you know that you desire to be in the presence of the object of your love more than the whole world. 'Love-sick' people are those who are unhappy because they are separated from the one they love. They have their money still, their books, their house and their friends, but they are love-sick and unhappy because the loved one is not there. You can offer them the whole world, but it is useless, for they only want their loved one. This is of more value to them than the whole of life.

Multiply that by infinity! This man has been in the presence of God. He has seen something of God's glory and he says, 'There is nothing which is of any value by contrast with this and nothing that I may receive from the whole universe is of any value compared with it.' There is a hymn by Augustus Toplady, which puts it very well:

> Object of my first desire;
> Jesus, crucified for me;
> All to happiness aspire,
> Only to be found in Thee:
>
> Thee to please, and Thee to know,
> Constitute my bliss below;
> Thee to see, and Thee to love,
> Constitute my bliss above.
>
> Lord, it is not life to live,
> If Thy presence Thou deny;
> Lord, if Thou Thy presence give,
> 'Tis no longer death to die.

You see, this means everything to him. It is because God is who and what He is. Once someone has had any knowledge of God, there is nothing else that comes into comparison, everything else pales and recedes into utter insignificance. And what David says is this: 'Oh, this knowledge is more precious to me than the whole of life, all of it put together.'

The second thing that makes David say this is that he has found a satisfaction in this intimate knowledge of God which completely satisfies him. 'My soul,' he says, 'shall be satisfied'—if I have this again—'with marrow and fatness.' That is a description of complete satisfaction and that is what the Christian finds in God and in the Lord Jesus Christ through the Holy Spirit. It is a complete satisfaction. The world cannot give it, but He gives it; He never fails. He satisfies the mind; He gives us understanding. Even in afflictions we are not perplexed, because we have this total, whole view of life; we know God's power and His purposes.

> Inspirer and hearer of prayer,
> Thou shepherd and guardian of Thine,
> My all to Thy covenant care,
> I sleeping and waking resign.
>
> Augustus Toplady

Christian men and women have light, even in the darkness. This, once more, is a great statement running through the Bible. Not only are their minds satisfied; their hearts are satisfied. For there is only one place where the heart can ever be at rest—it is in this intimate knowledge of God. 'The peace of God that passeth all understanding shall keep your heart and mind,' says the Apostle Paul. 'Be careful for nothing'—it does not matter where you are: in a wilderness; a dry and thirsty land with everything against you. 'Be careful for nothing'—do not be anxious—'but in everything by prayer and supplication with thanksgiving let your requests be made known unto God. And the peace of God which passeth all understanding shall keep your hearts and minds through Christ Jesus' (Phil 4:6–7).

This does not mean that you understand your circumstances fully, but that you have got peace in spite of them. Once you are with God you know that even though you do not understand, God understands. Like the little child who is perplexed and miserable, but when the father or mother comes, then the little child is perfectly happy. Why? Has it got understanding? No! It trusts the father and mother, they understand. And so true believers ever feel with God. They have peace and rest in their heart as well as understanding in their mind and their conscience is at rest. They are not troubled about their past and their sins and the fear of death. They know that all is well with their soul and well between them and God:

> If Thou art my shield and my sun,
> The night is no darkness to me;
> And, fast as my moments roll on,
> They bring me but nearer to Thee.
>
> Augustus Toplady

'To live is Christ and to die is gain!' Christians know this and that is why this is more valuable to them than anything else. And then Christians know, too, that this is something that can never change:

> Change and decay in all around I see,
> O Thou, who changest not, abide with me.
>
> Henry Francis Lyte

God is unchangeable. 'Thy lovingkindness is better than life,' says David. Not only that, David knows that God can vanquish all his enemies. He does think about them, but this is the answer to them: 'Those that seek my soul to destroy it, shall go into the lower parts of the earth, they shall fall by the sword: they shall be a portion for foxes...the mouth of them that speak lies shall be stopped.'

God is the all-powerful one. He can overcome all His enemies; nothing is impossible with Him, and so, surely, the one thing that matters is to be in this relationship with Him.

Then, David also knew that even should death come to him and his enemies be triumphant, it makes no difference to him; he will still be with God; he will see Him in the morning. 'Thy lovingkindness is better than life.' Why? Because he will behold the face of God: 'To die is gain!' So, obviously, this is of greater importance and of greater value to him than life itself, than the mere perpetuation of existence.

What else? Well, as the result of all this, of course, the Christian is someone who is filled with the spirit of thanksgiving and of praise and joy.

Because thy lovingkindness is better than life,
my lips shall praise thee.
Thus will I bless thee, while I live,
I will lift up my hands in thy name.
My mouth shall praise thee with joyful lips....
The king shall rejoice in God.

So how do you face up to this particular test? You believe in God, but do you praise Him? Do you thank Him? Do you rejoice in Him? 'The chief end of man is to glorify God and to enjoy Him for ever' (*The Shorter Catechism*). Are you enjoying Him? Do you thank Him? I am not asking if you believe in Him. I am asking if you know what it is at times for your heart to pour out in praise and in thanksgiving? David did, the children of God have ever done: 'Rejoice in the Lord alway and again, I say, rejoice!' says Paul to the Philippians.

Lastly, the Christian has a quiet confidence in God: 'Because thou hast been my help, therefore in the shadow of thy wings will I rejoice'; 'thy right hand upholdeth me.' That is the ultimate; knowing something of what it is to be 'under the shadow of His wings'. Have you seen those little chicks, playing about, pecking here and there, and then suddenly a dog or a cat appears and the little chicks all rush together to get under the shadow of the wing of the hen, their mother? Have you ever been in that shadow? Do you know what it is to feel the shadow of God's wings covering you, protecting you? Do you know that because you are His child that nothing can harm you, that the 'very hairs of your head are all numbered'? (Mt 10:30). For He has said, 'I will never leave thee nor forsake thee' (Heb 13:5). Do you know that He upholds you? That He will uphold you? And that He will never let you go?

There, then, are the marks, the signs and, therefore, the tests of the true man or woman of God. If that was true of David, how much more must it be true of us? In the light of Christ who has brought us nearer to Him, do we say, 'Thy lovingkindness is better than life'? Is our confidence in Him? Is God the supreme object of our desire? Can we say something like this?

O Lord, I would delight in Thee
And on Thy care depend,
To Thee in every trouble flee,
My best, my only, friend.

Notice this:

When all created streams are dried,
Thy fullness is the same,
May I with this be satisfied,
And glory in Thy name.

No good in creatures can be found
But may be found in Thee,
I must have all things and abound,
While God is God to me.

John Ryland

Is that your language? Do you honestly say,

Other refuge have I none,
Hangs my helpless soul on Thee,
Leave, ah! leave me not alone,
Still support and comfort me.
All my trust on Thee is stayed,
All my help from Thee I bring;
Cover my defenceless head
With the shadow of Thy wing.

Charles Wesley

Can you say that? That is the test: 'Thy lovingkindness is better than life'; or again, 'My soul longeth…my heart and my flesh crieth out for thee, the living God.'   Amen.

7   SEEKING CERTAINTY

O God, thou art my God; early will I seek thee:
my soul thirsteth for thee,
my flesh longeth for thee in a dry and thirsty land,
where no water is;
To see thy power and thy glory,
so as I have seen thee in the sanctuary.
Because thy lovingkindness is better than life,
my lips shall praise thee.

(PS 63:1–3).

ONCE AGAIN, I AM anxious to deal with the message of the entire psalm. We saw in our consideration of it in the last chapter that nothing matters, finally, save the knowledge of God. Here David has summed it up for us in this striking and wonderful phrase: 'Thy lovingkindness is better than life.' David does not plead for life, for what he wants is the lovingkindness of God. 'Having that,' he says, 'I am ready to face everything.' This is the most important thing in the whole of his experience.

Now this, surely, is the very essence of the Christian faith, something that we are all meant to have. It is not a mere head-theoretical knowledge, but a living vital experience of God through our Lord and Saviour Jesus Christ. And this is important, I want to suggest to you, for many reasons. Obviously, it is of supreme importance from the standpoint of personal experience. We are living in a difficult and a trying world, and we all, sooner or later, find ourselves in some kind of a wilderness, where nothing matters but this. When we are bereft of all the things that we normally have and enjoy: health, strength, wealth, friends or entertainment; when we are suddenly laid down by some serious illness, those things are of no help or value to us. We are just left alone and there nothing matters except our knowledge of God's lovingkindness:

> When other helpers fail and comforts flee,
> Help of the helpless, O, abide with me.
>> Henry Francis Lyte.

So, the real thing is that we should know always that He is there, that we have access to Him and that we can enjoy His presence in the most humbling, the most difficult, the most trying circumstances. It is the essence of wisdom from the standpoint even of personal experience.

But I have a second reason for emphasising this, which is that I am more and more convinced that this is the ultimate way of evangelism. There is a striking word in the Old Testament which tells us that many joined themselves to Judah, when they saw that God was with them. There had been a time of declension; people had been forgetting God and turning away from Him and so they had got into difficulties. Some had become cynical and were doubting and denying all their old faith and religion. But, something happened to certain people in Judah; they underwent a kind of reformation and revival. What we are told in Zechariah 8:23 is this: 'In those days it shall come to pass that ten men shall take hold of the skirt of him that is a Jew, saying, We will go with you; for we have heard that God is with you.' Now, I am quite sure that this principle operates today and will operate just as much as it did in those ancient times. In other words, I am certain that the way whereby we can attract the masses who are outside the church and outside Christ back to the faith is to show that God is with us. People are not interested in something theoretical. They have their own such interests and they can put that up against what we claim to believe. But the thing that always convinces people is reality. If they see that there is something about our lives, a certain quality, a certain calmness and equanimity, a certain ability to be more than conqueror in every kind of circumstance; if they see that when everything is against us, we still triumphantly prevail whereas they do not, then they will become interested in what we have. They will want to know more about it. I am convinced, therefore, that the greatest need today is for Christian people who know and manifest the fact that they know the living God and that to them His 'lovingkindness is better than life'.

In other words, there is nothing more important than assurance of salvation. It is the Christians who have assurance and peace and joy who have always been used by God in the propagation and the spreading of the truth. It is the great secret of triumphant living, but it is also the secret of true evangelism.

So we must now come to the very practical aspect of this matter and put it like this: how can we obtain this assurance if we do not already have it? Are we in this position? Can we say, with David, 'Thy lovingkindness is better than life'? Can we say, 'There is none other that I desire beside thee'? Have we this knowledge, this living, vital knowledge of God that David had, that Moses had, that the saints of the Bible have all had?

How can it be obtained? Here we are dealing with a most vital and important matter. The first answer I would give is that we must believe that it is possible for us. Obviously, that must come first. If you do not believe in this possibility then you will never seek it and obviously you will never find it. And there are many today who do not seek it because they do not believe in it. There are many who would regard this kind of thing as ecstasy or enthusiasm and they dislike it heartily and speak against it. Throughout the long history of the church, whenever something vital happens to individuals or to a group of people, when there is a kind of revival and reformation, the charge always brought against such people is 'enthusiasm'. The formal church never likes a living religion or a living faith, and it looks at it askance as something which is dangerous. 'This,' they say, 'is ecstasy; nothing but a riot of the emotions; this is something against which people should guard themselves.'

Now we all know the view which says that a Christian, after all, is someone who lives a decent life, who is a good fellow and who attends a place of worship now and again. But if you go beyond that and talk about some personal knowledge or experience, then you are not only regarded as being in a dangerous condition; some would even begin to doubt your very sanity. Take the remark made by Lord Melbourne, the nineteenth century Prime Minister: 'Things have come to a pretty pass if religion's going to start becoming personal!' You see, this objective, detached, theoretical view of the Christian faith dislikes a personal emphasis and especially a thrilling personal experience. Religion is that which makes a man decent, but nothing else beyond that.

Then there are others who do not seek this because they believe that this is something that belonged only to the New Testament times. You may say to them, 'But look here, go to the book of Acts and there you find the apostles on the day of Pentecost in such a condition that some people said they were drunk—'filled with new wine'. They were in a kind of ecstatic condition: filled with an exuberant joy and a spirit of exultation. 'Oh yes,' they say, 'that is all right, but that was the beginning of the church era, that is the book of Acts.' There is teaching at the present time which tells you not to pay too much attention to Acts. 'It is a dangerous book,' people say, 'to derive your doctrine from. You must not find it there.' So you discount most of what you read in Acts, saying that it was meant simply for those times and not for us.

Well, we have dealt with this argument elsewhere[1], but suffice it to say here that the answer to it is that you simply cannot understand the epistles except in the light of the background of the book of the Acts of the Apostles. You cannot read the epistles without seeing that there was this exuberance, this joy, this certainty, this knowledge and, therefore, it is a terrible thing to say that this was something that was only meant for New Testament times; indeed, it seems to me to come very near to quenching the Spirit.

Others are not interested in this vital knowledge of God because they dismiss it at once by saying, 'Oh, I do not dispute the validity of the experience, I am not denying that people like Moses and David and Paul and others have had these great experiences but, surely, this is only for certain, special people. It is not meant for everybody.' Now, the classic example of that mentality, of course, is what you get in the kind of churches which divide up the people into two groups—the religious and the ordinary—or the clergy, if you like, and the laity. They make their definite division. There is a kind of aristocracy, they say, in the Christian realm and in the church, and then there are the ordinary people. And, of course, the ordinary people are not meant to have these experiences or even to seek them. That is only for the Saints and only certain people are Saints. The church decides who is a Saint—they canonise the Saint—and he or she is always somebody quite exceptional. There are not many Saints, but the ordinary people—the rest of us—are not meant to be one of them.

So, of course, this teaching would automatically exclude this assurance. You just start by saying, 'Well, obviously, I'm not one of those special people; I'm a man of affairs and I've got to live my life in this world; I haven't got time to do this sort of thing. Of course, if I became a monk or something like that, then, no doubt, I should have these experiences, but I'm not called to that. I'm a kind of secular Christian, not one of these spiritual ones.' There are many who take up that attitude; it is a very pernicious teaching which easily insinuates itself. It is very subtle and so many Christian people say, 'No! It is not meant for all, it is only meant for certain, special people.'

The last reason I want to deal with is the one which is tremendously important at the present time, especially among those who belong to evangelical circles—it is the danger of what can most conveniently be described as 'Sandimanianism'. Now, let me expand that. There was a man called John Glas in Scotland towards the end of the eighteenth century, who had a son-in-law, an Englishman of the name of Sandyman. Together these men propounded a teaching that became tremendously popular and had a wide influence. It was to the effect that you need pay no attention whatsoever to your emotions in connection with your Christianity. They took the statement in Romans 10:9—'If thou shalt confess with thy mouth the Lord Jesus, and shalt believe in thine heart that God hath raised him from the dead, thou shalt be saved.' 'And that,' they said, 'is all you need do. If you say, in words, "I believe that Jesus Christ is the Son of God and that God raised Him from the dead,'' then you are saved, the Scripture says so. Feelings do not count at all, all you have to do is to believe the message and make that statement and then you are saved.'

That is what is meant by 'Sandimanianism'. It had a great popularity in the eighteenth century and it did very great harm. It wrought much havoc in the life of the church for many, many years afterwards. As a movement, it has virtually disappeared, but surely, the thing itself is very common. Is it not a very popular teaching nowadays? You are told the truth in a meeting and then you are asked in an enquiry room or somewhere, 'Do you believe that?'

'Yes!' you reply.

'Right,' they say, 'you're saved!' Simply because you say that you believe it!

But then you may say, 'But I don't feel anything, and I haven't felt any different.'

And their reply is: 'It doesn't matter at all! Don't worry about your feelings, it's a question of believing.'

So the whole emphasis in their teaching on conversion is put upon an intellectual belief, and if you can add to that that you have now tried to discipline your life a bit and that you have taken on a certain moral teaching such as is found in the Scriptures, you are regarded as a good and an excellent Christian and you do not need any more; you have received everything at that moment of conversion. The Holy Spirit has come to you in all His fulness, you do not, therefore, seek any more. So there you are; you have never felt anything at all, you have had no living experience of God or of Christ, but you say you believe and you are assured that you are all right.

And, of course, it has carried over to the whole doctrine of assurance. You go to such people, such teachers, and say to them, 'But I read of people who say that they have a great assurance of these matters.'

'That's all right,' this teacher replies, 'you should have assurance.'

'Well,' you respond, 'how can I get it?'

'Oh,' they claim, 'It's quite simple, come along.'

So they open up their Bibles to you and say, 'Now look at this: this is what the word of God says, "He that believeth on Him is not condemned, but he that believeth not [of course] is condemned already" (Jn 3:18). Do you believe that?'

You reply, 'Yes I do.'

'Very well,' they say, 'there it is, the Scripture gives you assurance!'

'But,' you protest, 'I don't feel anything!'

'But,' they insist, 'you're not meant to feel anything, you're just meant to believe the word of God.'

Now, this is a common teaching today with respect to assurance: it is all something which, you are told, you just take by faith. You are even discouraged from considering feelings; it is something objective, outside you. And so many people accept this, thinking that they have full assurance of salvation and that they have all that the New Testament and the Bible have to offer them.

But is there not something wrong here? Where is the knowledge of God? Where is the sense of awe? Where is this great thing found in the Bible, when men and women have known that they have been in the presence of the living God? Surely this is the explanation of the great difference between modern evangelicalism and that older evangelicalism that obtained until the middle of the last century? This is the great contrast, for instance, between today and the periods of the Protestant Reformers and the Puritans and the early Methodists, whatever their theological complexion might have been. Where has this sense of godliness gone, this sense of wonder and amazement and the 'joy unspeakable and full of glory'?

These, then, are some of the reasons why people do not seek this wonderful experience that came to Moses and to David and to others. They do not believe in it and because of this, they contradict the essential teaching of the Bible itself. The Bible never teaches a cold, intellectual believism but an experience which involves the whole person. It also teaches that this is something which is meant for all. The Bible nowhere confines this to a particular age or to a particular type of person or to select people only. The epistles are surely full of this: 'Rejoice in the Lord alway,' says the Apostle to the Philippians, 'and again, I say, rejoice' (Phil 4:4). Of course, this does not mean a sort of back-slapping, carnal joviality. You cannot imagine such things in connection with the Apostle Paul. No! It is a holy joy, a deep joy, like a mighty river flowing down to the sea.

Then the Apostle Paul tells the Ephesians—all the members of the church and the other churches to which that circular letter was obviously intended—that they, together with all saints everywhere, should know and learn 'the breadth, and length, and depth, and height; And to know the love of Christ which passeth knowledge, that ye might be filled with all the fulness of God' (Eph 3:18–19). Indeed, this is what we are all exhorted to know. I defy anybody to give me a scripture which says that this is only for some people. No, Christ died to bring all who believe in Him to God, to a living experience of Him. This is life eternal, He said, 'That they might know thee, the only true God, and Jesus Christ, whom thou hast sent' (Jn 17:3).

Or again, take the way in which the Apostle Paul puts it in Philippians 3. Here is a man who has believed for years, a great Apostle who has had wonderful experiences but who still says, 'That I might know Him...not as though I had already attained' (vs 10–12). He does not mean that he has no knowledge at all, but rather that he knows that he has not got it all and that he is not already perfect. He says, in effect, 'I want more, and more, and more of this.' And there he is, pressing after it: 'That I might know Him.' That does not mean knowing about Him. This word 'know' in the Bible has such a strong meaning and connotation; it means the knowledge of personal experience; it is experimental knowledge, through which we enter more deeply and profoundly into this blessèd experience of God.

Now the Bible offers this to all and sundry, all who are believers. This is what we are all expected to be like; and that is not only true in the teaching of the Bible; you will find that it has been true also in the subsequent history of the Christian church. Again, it applies to all types, all kinds, all ages, all countries, all climes, and all backgrounds. It is not confined to any age, nor to any type. This is the most wonderful, the most thrilling thing.

Let me just prove my contention by giving you just a few quotations. I want to show you now how this is true of people who may differ in their theology fundamentally and profoundly.

First, let me give you a quotation from a famous American called Cotton Mather. There was a great family in America from about the middle of the seventeenth century to the middle of the eighteenth century, the Mathers. One of them, Cotton, wrote a classic account of religion in the United States—*Magnalia Christi Americana*. Mather was an undoubted genius. He was brilliant as a boy, and his erudition was quite phenomenal. He was also a very great Calvinist in his theology, and this is how he writes in his diary in 1700. He had been passing through a time of difficulty and of trial. There was a particular problem pressing hard upon him and his father, Increase Mather, whose assistant he was. Cotton tells us that he had been actually prostrating himself on the floor, pleading with God.

Then this is how he goes on. 'All this while'—while he was pleading like this and praying—'my heart had the coldness of a stone upon it and the straitness that is to be expected from the bare exercise of reason.' His reason was quite clear, he was a minister, and a preacher and he believed the faith. There was no question about that. He had believed it since his very early youth and had been preaching it, but, he says, his heart was cold.

'But now,' he continues, 'all on the sudden, I felt an inexpressible force to fall on my mind, an afflatus that cannot be described in words. None knows it but he that has it. If an angel from heaven had spoken it articulately to me, the communication would not have been more powerful and perceptible. It was told me that the Lord Jesus Christ loved my father and loved me and that He took delight in us as in two of His faithful servants and that He had not permitted us to be deceived in our particular faith.'

There it is! There was a man who had believed everything that you can possibly believe, but his heart was cold. There was an absence of this sensible, living, realisation of God, but all of a

117

sudden, he says, it came, this 'afflatus'. He cannot describe it. He says, 'They alone know what it is who have experienced it.'

So there is one man. But now let me give you a very different type, a little extract from the diary of a man called Parkinson Milton who lived in the nineteenth century, up until about 1890. He was a very convinced Arminian—the exact opposite of the Calvinist, Mather. A man who was a primitive Methodist and who was regarded by many as a 'ranter', as the primitive Methodists often were, enthusiasts, people of ecstasy. Furthermore, he was born in very humble circumstances, very different from Cotton Mather. He was an able man but he lacked Mather's scholarship and erudition. But this is how he writes about himself on 26th October, 1874:

> My soul was, at times, in a burning rapture, almost too ecstatic for this tabernacle. Again and again I repeated the words such as in the martyrs glowed, dying champions for their God. The truth is, I had to cease doing so, feeling that the heavenly wine was too strong for the earthly vessel. Oh, when mortality shall be swallowed up of life! I burn for Christ. This soul, I offer, Christ, in flames to Thee, joy unspeakable and full of glory!

Now, these are but passing extracts. Let me put it in a rather more doctrinal manner. An early Puritan, William Ames, writes like this: 'The assurance of our calling and election is a thing greatly to be desired.' Now, these people knew all about the Scriptures and about taking the biblical evidence. But that is not what they are talking about. It is not just saying, 'There it is, do you believe that? Yes? Well, you've got full assurance.' No! 'The assurance of our calling and election is a thing greatly to be desired. This certainty is not only possible for us to attain unto but also it belongs to our duty to make our calling and election sure.'

Then listen to William Perkins, perhaps the first of the great Puritans at the end of the sixteenth century, who influenced most of the others: 'We do not teach that all and every man living within the precincts of the church professing the name of Christ is certain of his salvation, but that he ought so to be and must endeavour to attain there unto.' Now, that puts it quite clearly; you can be a Christian without it, but you have no right, in a sense, to be so. You ought to make certain of this. You can be a Christian without it, but it is your business to seek it and to obtain it, to possess it and to live in the full enjoyment of it.

Finally, let me put it to you in the form of a hymn. Here is another man, not as well known as those I have quoted, but he enjoyed the same experience:

> Loved with everlasting love,
>   Led by grace that love to know;
> Spirit, breathing from above,
>   Thou hast taught me it is so.

You see, it is the direct work of the Spirit, not this external, mere theoretical, intellectual assurance. That is all right, but if you stop short at that you are quenching the Spirit:

> O this full and perfect peace!
>   O this transport all divine!
> In a love which cannot cease
>   I am His, and He is mine.
>
> Heaven above is softer blue,
>   Earth around is sweeter green;
> Something lives in every hue,
>   Christless eyes have never seen:
> Birds with gladder songs o'erflow,
>   Flowers with deeper beauties shine,
> Since I know, as now I know,
>   I am His, and He is mine.

George Wade Robinson (1838–77)

I trust, then, that you are now convinced that this is something which we all ought to know and to possess. It is not confined to certain people, certain ages or certain places. It is meant universally for all God's children. God means His children to rejoice in Him. The Bible is full of that. 'The chief end of man is to glorify God and to enjoy Him for ever.' Are you enjoying God? We are meant to. Shame on us if we are not; still greater shame upon us if we try to dismiss that and say, 'As long as I believe and live a good life, surely, no more is demanded.' No, we are meant to rejoice in Him and to enjoy Him for ever.

How, therefore, is this to be obtained? Well, David answers the question for us. This is the gift of God, there is no question about that. But the fact that it is the gift of God does not mean that we do nothing. Rather, because we believe that it is His gift, we should be seeking it. The parent has the gift in his or her possession and the child knows it. Does that mean, therefore, that the child does nothing but just acts in a passive manner, hoping that the parent is going to give it? No, it asks, and asks and asks! And it keeps on asking and becomes a nuisance until it has got it. Indeed, this is what Scripture teaches. You cannot command it, nor can you take it by faith whenever you like. No, it is the sovereign gift of God, but that means that you should seek it.

Listen to David: 'O God, thou art my God; early will I seek thee.' There it is. He begins 'early'; he starts at once. He does not let any time pass at all. He starts to plead with God. That is the first thing; but I want to emphasise something further, which is that we should not only seek it 'early', but we should also seek it always. Here is an important practical point. So often, and I am sure we all plead guilty to this, we do this sort of thing in fits and starts. Something makes us aware of it and makes us desire it, so, at once, we seek it early—and then we begin to forget.

But David goes on, 'When I remember thee upon my bed and meditate on thee in the night watches.' You know, once men and women realise this possibility, it does indeed monopolise them. They have to do their work, of course, their business, their profession, whatever it is, and they must give their full minds to that. But during all their leisure time, this is the big thing, this is the thing that monopolises. And here, David says, in effect, 'Even when I am lying on my bed at night, that is the source, the ground of my meditation.' There is no doubt about this—once people have had a glimpse of these things, they become what has once been called 'God-intoxicated'. Count Zinzendorf said about himself, 'I have one passion: it is He and He alone.'

I have already used the analogy of human natural love. Let me use it again. When you are in that state of love, your mind is monopolised by the other person. If you wake at night, your mind goes to them. You are thinking about them and not about a thousand and one other things. No, when there is love you are monopolised, you are held as by a magnet and your mind is always there. That is what David says, 'I meditate on thee in the night watches...I remember upon my bed.' At all times, everywhere, he is meditating about this and seeking it. He does not merely start early, he keeps on and does it at all times.

Furthermore, I want to emphasise the eager aspect of this. You see how David goes from step to step? In verse 8 he says, 'My soul followeth hard after thee.' He is like a dog who has got a scent and who follows hard after the quarry. It is going ahead, but the dog is after it. Do we know anything about this eagerness? Is this the big concern, the big quest, the big passion of our lives? Read the biographies of the saints, like the people we have just considered, and you will find that they are eagerly seeking Him all the time. 'Oh that I knew where I might find Him,' says Job (23:3). 'This one thing I do,' says the Apostle Paul, 'forgetting those things that are behind...I press toward the mark' (Phil 3:13–14). It is this eagerness—'My soul followeth hard after thee' is how David puts it in this psalm—and it has always been a characteristic of the people who have come to rejoice in this, the highest blessing that the Christian salvation affords.

Then another very important element in this seeking is what I would call the element of recollection. David puts this in at least two different ways. In the second verse he says, 'To see thy power and thy glory, so as I have seen thee in the sanctuary.' And then in the seventh verse he says, 'Because thou hast been my help, therefore, in the shadow of thy wings will I rejoice.' This is a very important, practical principle. Did you notice that Cotton Mather wrote that his heart 'was like a stone'? We know about that, do we not? We believe the truth as it is in Christ Jesus, but what is our heart like? Someone once came to see me in my study—indeed it has happened to me many times—and he said, 'You know what bothers me? That I can sit and listen to what you have been saying about the Saviour and be so unmoved!' He believed it all, but he was not moved. There was no rapture; he felt that there should be and he was right. As Isaac Watts puts it in his great hymn:

> Love so amazing, so divine,
> Demands my soul, my life, my all.

So, then, what do you do when you are in such a state? Well, it is a very good thing to do what David did, to practise this art of recollection. It simply means that you remind yourself of what God has done for you in the past. Take up the slightest manifestation that you have ever had of the love of God; and remind yourself of it. Start with that and remind yourself of past blessings. The couplet in the well-known hymn puts it perfectly:

> Count your blessings, name them one by one;
> And it will surprise you what the Lord hath done.

You see, it is no use trying to work up your heart, to try to work up your feelings. People who do that in connection with religion are just displaying that they are ignorant of the whole thing. You cannot do it, but what you can do is to count your blessings. Just remind yourself of facts, things that have actually happened to you. Go over them, and as you do so you will find that your heart does begin to melt. But you have got to make the intellectual effort; you must exercise your will. You cannot just work, as it were, from nothing. Rather say, 'Now, this is what I *do* know,' and start from there.

Then you go from that and remind yourself of the promises of God. Read your Bible and you will find great promises there. Peter describes them as 'exceeding great and precious promises' (2 Pet 1:4)—and indeed they are. Go through them, make a list of them, put them down on paper if necessary and then, armed by these, go to God and plead them. Say, 'If enjoyment of you is possible, why do you not give it to me? You sent your Son into the world that I might know this, to bring me to you and to enable me to rejoice in you. I believe in Him, so in His name I pray, make this real to me. Grant me the Spirit in fulness. Shed your love abroad in my heart.' That is what is meant by recollection. You just remind yourself in that way. You remind yourself also of the being and the character of God. God is love, and He is more ready to give than we are to receive. It is all of grace. 'He has sent His only Son into this world'—that is the character of God.

So, then, if you do not know Him as you should, what is the matter? There must be something wrong with you. It makes you examine yourself and see your indolence; you see that you are like a spoilt child. You give all your time to other things; then you run and ask for a gift from your parent though you have not done what you were told to do. That is how we act with God. So having examined yourself, in humility and in contrition, helpless and hopeless, you will go to Him. You will open your heart and plead with Him. You will find that the hardness and the coldness have gone and that God will suddenly come and visit you. This is this great art of recollection: 'My soul thirsteth for thee, my flesh longeth for thee...To see thy power and thy glory, so as I have seen thee in the sanctuary.' Start with what you have got and then go through this process and it will lead you upwards and onwards.

Then, the last great principle which David teaches us here is the importance of praise and thanksgiving. Is this not one of the great lacks in our spiritual, our Christian lives? How little do we thank God! What little praise there is and adoration, what little pouring out of the heart in gratitude and in praise to Him for all His mercies! We are very ready to remind Him of things that have gone wrong. We are very ready to grumble and to complain. But how much do we praise God in our prayers, in our private devotions? How much does this element of praise come in?

The Apostle Paul, again, puts this so perfectly. In writing to the Philippians, he says, 'Be careful for nothing but in everything by prayer and supplication with thanksgiving let your requests be made known unto God. And the peace of God, which passeth all understanding, shall keep your hearts and minds through Christ Jesus' (Phil 4:6–7). This is the other aspect, of course, of 'count your blessings', and as you do so you must praise God and thank Him. Think of the human analogy. What do you think of a person who takes everything from you and never troubles to thank you? To take something for granted is a terrible thing. Apart from anything else, it is insulting, but what a poor kind of personality it indicates: someone who is always ready to hold out their hand and to take all, never troubling to thank or praise.

But is that not how we all treat God? If you want to know Him, if you want to know His smile, if you want to know something about this living realisation that God is your God and that He has loved you 'with an everlasting love', that you are His child and that He will 'never leave you nor forsake you'; if you want this living witness of the Spirit, this ultimate assurance which is the final assurance given by the Spirit of God Himself by the love shed abroad in your hearts, going upwards and back to Him in praise, worship, adoration and thanksgiving; if you want all that, then begin to praise God for what you have.

Praise Him for everything: for the gift of life and health and strength. There are many people who are ill and laid aside, and who cannot attend a place of worship. Do you thank God for your health and strength, your faculties, for all these gifts which He showers upon us so constantly and so freely. Thank God! David, of course, keeps on repeating this: 'Because thy lovingkindness is better than life, my lips shall praise thee. Thus will I bless thee while I live: I will lift up my hands in thy name...my mouth will praise thee with joyful lips.' And on he goes, even down to the last verse where he says, 'The king shall rejoice in God.'

There, then, is David's way of handling himself. A wilderness is a terrible place to be in. It is very miserable, it chills the heart and one feels cold. 'Very well,' says David, 'this is the thing to do.' And it is, my dear friends, still the thing to do. If that was true of David, if he and others in the Old Testament could rejoice like that and enjoy God, how much more so should we who have the knowledge of Christ Jesus and His great salvation and all that has been made possible through Him. They simply saw it afar off, but we look back upon it. We know that it is a fact and that this Forerunner has entered for us into heaven and is appearing on our behalf at the right hand of God.

Give Him, therefore, no rest until He has satisfied the longing of your heart. Until you know, as these others have known, that 'I am His and He is mine.' Take up that word of Isaiah: 'Ye that make mention of the Lord, keep not silent and give him no rest, till he establish and till He make Jerusalem a praise in the earth' (Is 62:6–7). You give Him no rest until you have this blessèd knowledge. Or take a word again from Psalm 81. It is a wonderful expression and I feel we all need its exhortation. Psalm 81:10—'I am the Lord which brought thee out of the land of Egypt, open thy mouth wide and I will fill it.' Is your mouth wide open? Or have you got a nice, smug, little evangelicalism which does not expect anything further, which tells you that you have had it all at your rebirth and conversion. The answer is 'open your mouth wide' and let something of the fulness of God enter in.

Oh, this pernicious doctrine, this Sandimanianism, this modern version of it that keeps it entirely to the mind and is not interested in the heart and even distrusts warmth and emotion. It is so afraid of excesses that it quenches the Spirit, God have mercy upon it! Listen to God speaking to you and this is what He says, 'Hear, O my people and I will testify unto thee, O Israel, if thou will hearken unto me.' Then God, as it were, goes on and complains, 'O, that my people had hearkened unto me and Israel had walked in my ways; I should soon have subdued their enemies, and turned my hand against their adversaries. The haters of the Lord should have submitted themselves unto him: but their time should have endured forever. He should have fed them also with the finest of the wheat; and with honey out of the rock, should I have satisfied thee' (Ps 81:13–16).

Have you tasted of this honey from the rock? Is your heart, is your soul satisfied? Open your mouth wide and let Him fill it with the unsearchable riches of Christ; the knowledge of God; the 'joy unspeakable and full of glory'. Let me urge you again to listen to the advice of William Carey and 'Expect great things from God'.

> Thou art coming to a King,
> Large petitions with thee bring,
> For His grace and power are such,
> None can never ask too much.

John Newton.

So go on asking that you may know Him, with a personal intimate knowledge that will ravish your heart; go on asking until you have received. 'Ask.... Seek.... Knock...and it shall be opened unto you' (Lk 11:9).   Amen.

---

1. *Joy Unspeakable* (Kingsway: Eastbourne, 1985).

8   *ALWAYS IN HIS PRESENCE*

> I have set the Lord always before me:
> Because He is at my right hand,
> I shall not be moved.
> (PS 16:8).

I CALL YOUR ATTENTION to this verse, in order that by means of it and its teaching we may consider our lives together in this world as Christian people; that we may find guidance and help as we face the future, and that we may remind ourselves of certain things that are of vital importance to our souls and their eternal salvation. Here we have a man, the psalmist, telling us how he faces the future. It is a psalm of David and David was a man of like passions with ourselves. He had many troubles, he had to face many problems. He brought many of them upon himself, as we do; but many came in spite of him, just as the result of the world in which he lived and just because there were other sinners like himself all around him. If you read his story, you will find that he lived a very tempestuous kind of life. And yet through it all, with all his sins and faults and failures, and all the various calamities that came to meet him, you find this man going steadily forward; a man who was well pleasing in God's sight, a writer and a composer, author of many of these great psalms in which he celebrates God's goodness and lifts up his heart in praise.

Such a man, obviously, has a great deal to teach us and here he tells us one of the secrets of his life, one of the things that kept him going. He shows us what it was that enabled him to recover himself when he fell into sin or when he was indeed almost overwhelmed by trouble. It is always a good thing to pay very careful attention to any statement made by such a man. There is nothing that I know of, next to the reading of the Scriptures themselves, which is more profitable in the Christian life than a careful, constant reading and study of Christian biography. And, of course, the book of Psalms is pre-eminent in that very respect. The psalmist opens his heart to us; and here, in this one verse, he holds us face to face with what was, after all, the grand secret of the life of David, the king of Israel.

But, and this is a very important addition, this particular psalm is one of the so-called 'Messianic' psalms, one of the prophecies of the coming of the Messiah, the Son of God. Now, those who are familiar with their New Testaments, as all ought to be, will know that this psalm is quoted very frequently here with respect to our Lord Himself, and especially with respect to His resurrection. Take these words: 'thou wilt not leave my soul in hell neither wilt thou suffer thine Holy One to see corruption'. That was quoted by Peter on the day of Pentecost, by Paul in Antioch of Pisidia, and it was quoted again in the Epistle to the Hebrews. It is, undoubtedly, a reference to the Lord Jesus Christ.

So David, here, was not only writing about himself; he was writing as a prophet about the 'Coming One', the Son of God, the Messiah, and therefore, these words can be appropriated to our Lord Himself. In other words, we have in this verse not only, if I may so put it, the secret of the life of King David, we have also the essence and the secret of the life of our blessed Lord and Saviour Jesus Christ, the Son of God, when He was here in this world and lived His life as a man. 'I have set the Lord always before me.' That was how He lived. As you read the accounts of His life, which you will find in the four gospels, you will find that this is obviously true. Observe His life of prayer. See Him getting up before dawn to pray or spending a whole night in prayer. What is He doing? Why is he praying so much? He is setting the Lord always before Him. It is perfectly clear from the gospels that our Lord, when He was here in the flesh, lived in that way. He looked to God; He lived for Him and by Him.

We see here, then, that we have a most important ruling and principle with regard to our lives in this world. Nothing can be more important than this: the secret of the life of David, indeed, of the human life of the Lord Jesus Christ. Again, if you read Christian biographies you will find that it has also been the characteristic note, the outstanding feature in the life of all men and women who have had unusual experiences of the grace of God and who have been used by Him in an exceptional manner in their lives and ministries.

So let us, therefore, consider our own lives. How do we feel as we look into the future? What is going to happen? I do not know; nobody else knows, and I shall not waste your time in trying to predict what will happen, or in telling the politicians and the statesmen what they ought to do in order to govern the future. I am in no position to do that and I know of nobody else who occupies a pulpit, whatever position he may hold as an ecclesiastic, who is in a position to do so. No, I have a much higher calling. My business is to prepare you for whatever may happen. We do not know what that may be. Look back over the past year and consider the things that have happened to you. How many of them did you predict? How many of them did you anticipate?

I thank God that as Christian people, we do not need to know the future. Christians should never have that desire to know. Christians live in this way: 'one step enough for me'. And not only that, they have this principle, if they put it into operation, which will enable them to say, 'Whatever happens to me I know that all will be well, because "He is at my right hand, I shall not be moved". Come what may, "I shall not be moved" because I am living in the light of this principle, that "I have set the Lord always before me".' Let us, then, look at this verse in a very practical manner.

Now I say that quite deliberately. The principles are here, of course, and we should spend a great deal of our time with principles and with doctrines, because they are absolutely essential. But, obviously, they must be applied and, therefore, it is not a bad thing, occasionally, to pause and be essentially practical, to come down to the application of the things which we have seen together and which we most surely believe. What then, is the practical approach to this whole teaching? It is the determination to live life in the conscious presence of God. That is what the psalmist is saying. He has set the Lord God always before him; he says, 'I'm going to live in that way consciously as in His presence; as long as I do that, I shall never be moved.'

This is the supreme object of David's life and he emphasises that by the words that he uses; you notice how he puts it: 'I have *set* the Lord always before me'. That is an extraordinary term to use and I have no doubt that at first sight when we look at it and read it, it comes to us rather as a surprise. Here is a man who says that he is going to '*set*' God before him. But what does he mean by this? How can a mortal man thus manipulate, as it were, or '*set*' God?

That is what we feel at once and yet we know that that is not what David had in his mind. No, what David was really saying was that he was going to set himself in the presence of God. It is just a human way of speaking. We say to ourselves, 'I must remind myself about this, I must put up a notice in front of me in order that I shall not forget it, I must set it in front of me.' That is the idea. What David really means is that he is going to bring himself into that position; 'I have set the Lord.' It is a term which is used very frequently in the Scripture. We see it, for instance, in the Epistle to the Colossians, because there we find the other side of it emphasised. Paul, addressing these Christian people, says, 'Set your affections on things above, not on things on the earth' (Col 3:2). We should set ourselves in the right angle, in the correct position; we must get the right perspective; we must constantly look at those things and gaze upon them.

David rather puts it the other way round but it is exactly the same thing. It is the term itself, however, that is so important for us as we come down to the practicalities of this matter, so I make no apology at all for breaking it up very simply into its component parts. '*Setting*' obviously implies a determination. It includes an act of the will. It implies a very definite decision. Take an ordinary domestic illustration: you *set* your alarm clock to go off at a certain time in the morning. Now obviously, before you actually do it, you must have decided to do so. You have said, 'I want to wake up at a given time in the morning and therefore I am going to set my alarm clock at that given point.'

It is the same idea here. It involves determination and, of course, determination involves thought. It involves meditation and consideration. This is the end of an argument, the outcome of a great process of reasoning on David's part. It is the implementation of a point of view with regard to himself and with regard to the whole of life; having considered everything, this is the way he is going to live. He has determined it.

And we, too must determine. We must decide. We must exercise our will power. I am referring here, of course, to the whole tendency to drift and to allow life to manipulate us and to carry us along. I am sure that as we examine ourselves at this moment; as we look back across our past life, we must be more alarmed at that than at any other single matter, namely, the way in which the months and the years are passing and we have not done what we proposed to do. As Milton put it in his great sonnet,

> When I consider how my life is spent
> Ere half my days in this dark world and wide.

He felt that he had wasted his life; he had not done things and his blindness had come upon him.

And I am sure that we all must feel something like that. We are so busy, there are so many things to do, never has life been more difficult. Life seems to be organised for us and the most difficult thing in the world is just to isolate ourselves and to insist upon controlling our lives, living them as we believe they should be lived. We have got to decide; we must determine, because if we do not, our lives will be governed by the round, by the circle in which we live. The newspapers will come in and we will start with them at breakfast; then other things will come, business and friends and affairs and meetings and so on. And we are all so busy with such things that we almost forget our immortal soul. 'I have set'. I am determined; I am resolved; I will! That is the first thing.

But, at the same time, I must emphasise the element of activity in this, and here again is something very vital. We must rouse ourselves and bring ourselves to this. Here is a point which, to me at any rate, is of very great interest. There are two sides to this Christian life in which we find ourselves. There is the divine initiative without which nothing happens at all. But, as the result of that divine initiative, we are meant to initiate things ourselves. When we are dead in trespasses and sins we can do nothing, but when we are given life, we can, and we must, and the Scriptures appeal to us to do so: '*set* your affections'. We must take ourselves in hand and make ourselves do this. We must compel ourselves; be rigid with ourselves; discipline ourselves. It involves a very definite activity on our part.

I am putting it like this because I know that there are some of us who tend perhaps to take the view that, well, we just go on as we are and we pray that God will do something to us. We are waiting for a revival or some personal revelation and, in the meantime, we tend to do nothing. Now that is quite false to the scriptural teaching. We cannot create a revival, it is folly to attempt to do so, but there is a great deal we can and must do. We must not just get up in the morning and say, 'Well, I don't feel in a very spiritual mood this morning, I trust that I shall be better tomorrow.' Not at all! 'I have set the Lord always before me.' When we feel the exact opposite, we must insist upon it. We must do this thing; we must take ourselves in hand; we must set Him before us and speak to Him.

That is what David means; it is an activity. It is not only waiting passively for the Lord graciously to visit us. He does that, but Christian biography proves abundantly that the people who have had the most gracious and the most frequent visitations from God have been those who have sought Him most diligently. The author of the Epistle to the Hebrews says, 'He that cometh unto God must believe that He is and that He is a rewarder of *them that diligently seek Him.*' That is the activity that we must undertake.

The next step is still more practical. Setting the Lord before me means that I train and school myself in what the masters of the spiritual life have called 'the art of recollection'. It means that I consciously, deliberately and actively speak to myself about myself and about my relationship to God. It means that when I wake up in the morning, before I allow myself to think about anything else, I say to myself, 'You are a child of God and an heir of eternity; God knows you and you belong to Him'—recollection! Now, I must do that, and do it forcibly, because the moment I wake up thoughts will come crowding into my mind, perhaps temptations, perhaps doubts; all sorts of things. But I brush them all aside and deliberately remind myself of God and myself and my relationship to Him. And I meditate upon that and then I consciously seek the presence of God. To put it another way, I must 'practise the presence of God'.

In other words, I say to myself, God is and I am, and God is there. God is eternal being and life and reality. He is not a mere term or a philosophic concept—God *is*. He is a Person, and I want to go into His presence. I want to know Him; I want to speak to Him. I am going to approach Him, as I may decide to visit a friend. I am going to visit God and commune with Him; I am going to have fellowship with Him. That is what David means by setting the Lord always before Him.

Of course, there are many other ways of doing this. Nothing is more important than this word, the Bible. God has revealed Himself to us there, so as we read it, we are deriving knowledge about God. He is speaking to us through the Word about Himself and about ourselves, so that the more we know it and read it, the more it will take us into the presence of God. So if you want to set the Lord always before you, spend much of your time with regular daily reading of the Bible. And let it be systematic reading, not picking it up at random and turning, perhaps to a favourite psalm and then to somewhere in the gospel. No, it must be Genesis to Revelation! Go through the Book year by year. I think any Christian should be ashamed who does not go through the Bible once a year. Go through it systematically. There are many schemes that have been designed and which can be purchased which will tell you how to do it and help you to do so. Or, if you like, you can work one out for yourself as I once did. But whatever you do, insist upon it. Here is God's word! He is speaking to you—listen to Him and you will come into His presence. Set Him before you by reading the Bible.

Then, there is prayer; talking to God and listening to Him. Those are the ways in which you set Him before you, and, too, I must repeat, read the lives of godly people. When you see the kind of life that they were enabled to live, you will feel, 'Oh that I were like that!' You will discover that the reason for their living as they did was that they always set the Lord before them. And so you read that when they were taken desperately ill, or when bereavement and sorrow came, it did not disturb their equanimity, they were not finally upset. They were not inhuman, they did feel these things and they felt them very acutely; but they did not lose their balance. They did not feel that all was lost and gone. And when wars came, and trials and calamities, they did not feel that everything had collapsed. Not at all! They went on and there was a kind of added sweetness and beauty about their lives and a still greater joy and peace. That is what you find as you read their biographies, and you will find that their secret was that they spent a great deal of time every day in reading the Scriptures and in praying to God.

My dear Christian friends, is this not the trouble with so many of us today? We are much too busy; we are activists. We are running to meetings or organising them or busying ourselves in various organisations. We do not read even, as our forefathers did. We must always be entertained, we must be looking at something, or somebody must be doing it for us. The secret of the saints in the past was that they read the word themselves and prayed and meditated and read good books. Not snippets, not mere devotional commentaries; they got down to the doctrine, to the depths, and they lived in these depths and not merely in the shallows. And the result was their glorious lives.

Oh that we may all resolve to be like that! Do not let life control you. Never let any organisation control you. Do not let 'the thing to do' control you, and when I say that, I do not only mean it as it applies in the world. I mean 'the thing to do' even in evangelical circles. Set the Lord always before you, the Lord Himself—not merely activities in His kingdom; because, finally, if you do not do this, you will become very dry in all your activism. Your heart will become cold, and in the time of need and of trouble and of trial you will not know where you are and you will be rather a poor witness to the faith and to the grace which you have received and which you hold.

'I have set the Lord *always*,' says David; not only when he feels like it. We must do this still more, in a sense, when we do not feel like it. When the Lord is visiting us, we need not set Him before us, we know that He is there and we have got to respond. No, the time to do it is when we do not feel it, and when we feel dry and barren and arid—then we must set Him before us. Surely we must all testify to the fact that as we look back across our lives, there is nothing, in a sense, that has been more wonderful than when in an arid and barren condition, we have deliberately set Him before us and sought Him. Suddenly the clouds have broken and the light has shone again. Oh, there has been nothing more wonderful than that! So do it, even though you do not feel like it, do it every day. Always! Do not do it fitfully, do not start off wonderfully and then begin to flag. Always! Set your affections—put them there, put them at that point and keep them there. Go on doing it.

And above all, do not only do it when you are in trouble, which is the tragedy with so many. They have gone on living a humdrum life, saying, 'Of course, should things go wrong, I can always turn to the Lord.' And then things have gone wrong, and they have turned to Him, but they have rather felt that they could not find Him. So they seem to be deserted and then they become excited and alarmed and do not know where they are. They only set the Lord before them when they are in trouble. But if you want to find the Lord when you are facing difficulties, then set Him before you when you are not. Sunshine and rain; storm and calm; affluence and prosperity, penury and loss; health and sickness, you will not care, because you have set the Lord *always* before you.

Shall I encourage you by reminding you of the wisdom of doing this? I have referred to it already, but let me emphasise it. Why should I set the Lord always before me? First, because He is the Lord Jehovah, the almighty, the eternal, the everlasting God. If that is not enough, the second reason is: because I am always before Him. He is the Lord; and there are statements in Scripture, anthropomorphic statements, but how true and how expressive, which say that the 'eyes of the Lord...run to and fro through all the earth' (Zech 4:10). He sees; He knows all and everything. And because His eye is always upon me, it is the essence of wisdom that my eye should be always upon Him. 'All things are naked and opened unto the eyes of Him with whom we have to do' (Heb 4:10). Nothing is hidden from His sight.

And indeed, that brings me to the third reason. I should 'set the Lord always before me' because it is as certain as the fact that I am on earth at this moment, that I shall one day stand before God. When, I do not know; so, therefore, let me always do it. Not one of us knows when, but we do know this for certain; that we shall all appear before the judgement seat of Christ and 'give an account of the deeds done in the body' (Rom 14:12). It is inevitable, it is inexorable, therefore, my dear friend, set the Lord always before you! It is the essence of wisdom to do this; rehearse it if you like.

But now, let us look briefly at the privilege of doing this. What poor and foolish creatures we are! Yet the essence of Christianity is to bring us into fellowship with God. By living, by dying on the cross and by rising again, what Christ has made possible by all that, is that you and I can live and walk in that fellowship. Enoch walked with God, so did Noah. Abraham, the friend of God, walked with God, and you and I are meant to walk with Him through this world. What a privilege! And it is a tragedy that we have to remind ourselves of it, but we must. Do it always. Set Him always before you. Say, as you wake up in the morning, 'What a wonderful thing, another day of walking with God! Walking with Christ! Our fellowship indeed is with the Father and with His Son, Jesus Christ!' Oh, if we started our days like that! Reminding ourselves of that, miserable creatures such as we are, feeling jaded, tired, bilious, depressed, whatever it is, with all sorts of thoughts and problems coming; brush them all aside and say, 'It's God's day and I am God's child! I am going to walk with Him today!' That is the Christian life.

Then, finally, a word about the comfort of setting the Lord always before us. The comfort and the security of doing so, because it is as certain as we live, that as we start any day, we shall find ourselves face to face with temptations. There is an adversary confronting us who is second only to God in power, a mighty adversary—'a roaring lion, seeking whom he may devour' (1 Pet 5:8), and he will attack us with all his power. There is only one comfort as we realise something of the truth of that. It is that we can say,

> I need Thee every hour,
> Stay Thou near by.

Why? Well

> Temptations lose their power
> When Thou art nigh.
>
> Annie Sherwood Hawks (1835–1918)

If the Lord is before you when the temptation comes, it will be quite different from facing it alone and not knowing that He is there. Indeed, it seems to me on reflection, that those who start the day without realising all this, and without setting the Lord before them are fools. They are child's play to the devil. So make certain that you have set the Lord before you. And keep it up.

Then think of trials when they come. They may come in so many different forms: increasing age, infirmity, sickness, the sickness of someone else, bereavement, sorrow, perhaps a war, the collapse of the world and civilisation, we do not know. But they may come. They will come sooner or later in some way. And then, you know, there is only one thing that is of value, and that is that we shall not be alone, that He will be with us. The Lord Jesus Christ said to His disciples, 'The hour cometh and is now come that ye shall be scattered, every man to his own, yet I am not alone, because the Father is with me' (Jn 16:32). That is how He went through it all. When His disciples ran away—'the Father is with me'—and He went on. And that is the only way in which you and I can face it. We can say this:

His oath, His covenant, His blood;
Support me in the whelming flood.
When all around my soul gives way,
He only is my strength and stay.
On Christ, the sold rock, I stand,
All other ground is sinking sand.

Edward Mote (1797–1874)

Ah, yes, and when even death itself shall come, it is all right. He will be with us, He will not leave us, nor forsake us. We can apply this psalm. Christ has conquered death and the grave; He has gone through. He is an 'anchor within the veil' (Heb 6:19). Because He is there, I shall be there. Even death is vanquished.

And the glory of it is this: I know that I am changeable; but I know that He is unchangeable. The world will change and I will change. He, Christ, is 'the same yesterday, today and forever' (Heb 13:8). Therefore, whatever may happen, I have but to set Him always before me, and to look at Him. I seek Him and ask Him to abide with me and therefore I can say things like this:

Abide with me: fast falls the eventide,
The darkness deepens; Lord, with me abide:
When other helpers fail, and comforts flee,
Help of the helpless, O abide with me.

Swift to its close ebbs out life's little day;
Earth's joys grow dim, its glories pass away;
Change and decay in all around I see:
O Thou who changest not, abide with me.

I need Thy presence every passing hour;
What but Thy grace can foil the tempter's power?
Who like Thyself my guide and stay can be?
Through cloud and sunshine, O abide with me.

I fear no foe, with Thee at hand to bless;
Ills have no weight, and tears no bitterness:

Where is death's sting? Where, grave, thy victory?
I triumph still if Thou abide with me.

Hold Thou Thy cross before my closing eyes,
Shine through the gloom, and point me to the skies;
Heaven's morning breaks, and earth's vain shadows flee:
In life, in death, O Lord, abide with me.

Henry Francis Lyte (1793–1847)

Beloved friend, set the Lord always before you and then because He is at your right hand, you will not be moved.   Amen.

9 SEEKING THE FACE OF GOD

Psalm 27

A PSALM, WE MUST always remember, is a song and it is, therefore, something which should usually be taken as a whole, because generally, in that song, the psalmist has one great message to give us. That is particularly true of this twenty-seventh psalm, but we can perhaps look at that one verse in particular—verse 4.

> One thing have I desired of the Lord,
> that will I seek after;
> that I may dwell in the house of the Lord,
> all the days of my life,
> to behold the beauty of the Lord,
> and to enquire in his temple.

Now, as in most of the psalms, the psalmist here is giving us his experience, because he is anxious to praise God. He is also anxious to help others. For that is the whole purpose of giving an experience, not to call attention to oneself but to call attention to the Lord who is the giver of all experiences and who alone is worthy to be praised. And as we look at the experience of this man we can learn many lessons from him, because he is teaching us here how to face the whole problem and battle of life and of living.

That is the great value, of course, of the psalms; they are always so practical because they are experimental or experiential. They have this additional value, that it is not a man writing theoretically about life; it is generally someone who, having passed through some experience which tried and tested him, has again discovered the way of success and of triumph. So he wants to celebrate that and to pass on the information to others. And another great value, of course, of the psalms is the fact that they are always so honest. The psalmist does not pretend that he is better than he is. He opens his heart; he exposes himself to us, as it were, exactly as he is. He tells us about his fears and his forebodings; he never conceals any of his own weaknesses and so we feel that he speaks to our condition.

As far as this psalm is concerned, no one can decide for certain whether the psalmist wrote it immediately after a great trying experience or whether he wrote it while he was actually facing some such trial. It is probably a psalm of David, and therefore we can assume that as David was constantly suffering troubles and tribulations, then he is telling us of some very recent experience in this psalm.

Now, the value of all this to us is obvious, because, after all, in our daily lives each of us is involved in struggle. Nothing is so wrong, and indeed dishonest, as to pretend that the moment you become a Christian all your problems are left behind and that you will never have any difficulties any more. That is just not true. The Christian is not promised an easy time in this world, indeed, the reverse is much nearer the truth. We are told in many places in the New Testament that because we are Christians we can expect unusual trials precisely because we are followers of the Lord.

Look at His life. There He was, the Son of God in this world; yet He was tried; He was tempted; He was tested; He had to suffer the contradiction of sinners against Himself. His life was one of battle and of conflict; and if that was true of Him, as He Himself pointed out in John 15, how much more is it likely to be true of His followers? Because we are Christians, the devil and all his forces will be particularly concerned to try us and to test us; to bring us down, if not into sin, at any rate into a condition of defeat and of unhappiness, filled with a sense of insecurity and a spirit of fear.

So the New Testament, as well as the Old, prepares us for all that. God's people have had great trials and tribulations and fights while they were in this world. We are not promised an easy time, but what we are assured is that in spite of it all, we can be 'more than conquerors'. That is the Christian position. It does not minimise the problems, nor does it tell us that there will be none, rather it faces them as they are. Indeed, I have often claimed that the Bible is the most honest book in the world. It is the politicians, the philosophers and the poets who are always promising us that our troubles will be abolished. These are the dangerous optimists, these idealists, who are always going to make a perfect world.

The Bible never says that. The Bible tells us the precise opposite; it says that while men and women are in rebellion against God and are sinners, the world will be full of problems and difficulties. Yes, there will be 'wars and rumours of wars' (Mk 13:7). The Bible has always said that. It is other people, those who do not believe the Bible, who promise that by some human organisation we will banish war. But the Bible is realistic and tells us that there are enemies and powers set against us, but that in spite of that we can be 'more than conquerors through Him that loved us' (Rom 8:37).

So, how are you standing up to life? How are you getting on in this battle? Are you triumphant, are you assured? That is what we are meant to be as God's people. How are you facing the stresses and the trials, the troubles and the tribulations of life? Well, in this psalm we turn to the right way of facing these problems because here, the psalmist tells us, out of his own experience, the only way whereby we can indeed truly do so in a world like this.

Here, then, is a psalm of some fourteen verses which can be divided up simply into three sections. In the first section, verses 1 to 6, the psalmist expresses his confidence, his assurance. Then in the second section, verses 7 to 12, he comes to petition, to prayer, out of the midst of the struggle and the conflict and the agony. And then, in verses 13 and 14, he arrives at his final conclusion with regard to this whole matter. Or, to put it in another way, in the first section the psalmist is in heaven, in the second section he is very much down to earth, and in the third section he gives us his decision with regard to the whole of his future and as to how life is to be faced.

So what we have here in this psalm is what we may well call 'a strategy for living', how to face the battle and the conflict in life. As you know, you must always start with strategy not with tactics, because if you do not you will soon find yourself defeated. You may think you are getting a little victory here, but you have forgotten something else. So you must start with a grand strategy of life and that is stated to perfection here in this one psalm. It is that we must always start in heaven and with God. Then, having done that, we come down to earth and face the problems of life and of living as we find them in the light of what we have already seen in heaven with God.

That, then, is the great principle, and we all get into trouble because we forget this essential strategy. Never start with your problems, never! Never start with earth; never start with men. Always start in heaven; always start with God. That is really the one great message of the psalm, but the psalmist puts it, of course, in different ways. He puts it in this experiential form so that he is very much with us and one of ourselves. But this is the essential principle, and if we do not grasp it, there is no point in continuing. The one thing with which we must always start is our relationship to God. The whole trouble in the world today is due to the fact that that has been forgotten. People always start with themselves, with the world, with life, and with their problems. This is true of all who are not Christians and that is why they never succeed. They have already started in a wrong way and it must inevitably lead to failure.

So having established the strategy in our minds, let us follow the psalmist as he works this out for us. Pay attention to him and ask God to give you His Spirit, so that you may understand this most precious truth which can revolutionise your whole life and your outlook upon it. Do you feel defeated, frightened, fearful of life? My dear friend, here is the very thing you need. Take heed for all you are worth, for all your life, and this man will show you how to be 'more than conqueror'.

We start, therefore, with the psalmist's confidence:

> The Lord is my light and my salvation;
> whom shall I fear?
> the Lord is the strength of my life;
> of whom shall I be afraid?
> When the wicked, even mine enemies and my foes,
> came upon me to eat up my flesh,
> they stumbled and fell.

And, notice this:

> Though an host should encamp against me,
> my heart shall not fear:
> though war should rise against me,
> in this will I be confident.

Then he goes on in the fifth verse:

> For in time of trouble He shall hide me in His pavilion:
> in the secret of His tabernacle shall He hide me;
> He shall set me up upon a rock.
> And now shall mine head be lifted up
> above mine enemies round about me.

So he ends by saying, 'I will sing, yea, I will sing praises unto the Lord.'

Now, this is tremendous confidence. He says, in effect, 'I am not afraid, nor is there any need to be afraid. Even though my enemies shall all gather and conspire together and come upon me all at the same time, it does not matter. Let war rise against me, I am not going to be afraid. Nothing can ever defeat me, whatever it may chance to be.' Now, this is overwhelming assurance, and it is, of course, typical of the attitude of these men of God that we read of in the Bible from the very beginning to the very end.

If you want a kind of corresponding statement in the New Testament, then consider the end of that great eighth chapter of Paul's Epistle to the Romans, where the Apostle, having given a list of his trials and troubles and tribulations, saying that we are led every day as 'sheep to the slaughter', comes to this conclusion: 'For I am persuaded'—I am certain—'that neither death, nor life, nor angels, nor principalities, nor powers, nor things present, nor things to come, nor height, nor depth, nor any other creature, shall be able to separate us from the love of God, which is in Christ Jesus our Lord' (vs 38–39).

'I know! I am certain!' There is the great Christian note: facing life at its very worst, yet there is no fear, no uncertainty. There is no shrinking or trembling, as you look at this unknown future. Not at all! What ever it may be, I am confident! I am persuaded! I am certain! I am sure!

Now, these things are not theoretical, and you and I are men and women living in the midst of life; so have you got this confidence? Are you facing life like this? Are you able to face the future, whatever it may be, and say, 'I know, I am certain, I shall not fear, whatever may happen; in this I am confident'?

But then, we must ask a question: what is the source of this man's confidence? Is it just foolhardiness, some kind of braggadocio? Is he a man we can listen to? He is, of course, because he is so honest; he is not merely making wild statements. We have known people like that, have we not? We remember the Apostle Peter telling our Lord that though all men would desert Him, he would never do so, yet in a few hours he was denying Him in base cowardice.

But this is very different—on what does the psalmist base his confidence? What is the source of his great assurance? Well, he tells us quite plainly that it is nothing in himself, nothing at all. That is the meaning of this extraordinary thirteenth verse which reads in the Authorised Version: '*I had fainted*, unless I had believed to see the goodness of the Lord in the land of the living.' Now, the words '*I had fainted*' are in italics because they are not in the original. They have been supplied, and rightly so, by the translator. For the psalmist is writing under the stress of a great emotion. He remembers the terrible predicament that he was in, the forces that were against him, and his consciousness of his own weakness, so he just blurts out, 'Unless I had believed to see the goodness of the Lord....' And he just leaves it like that—I would have been completely undone; I would have been filled with despair; 'I would have fainted'.

Here, you see, is the starting point and we must not forget it. This man is not a mere boaster, a braggart. He is not just a foolish man who has confidence in himself and who says that he does not care what life may bring against him, because he is so sure and certain of himself. He does not write like the poet at the end of the last century:

> It matters not how straight the gate,
> How charged with punishment the scroll,
> I am the master of my fate,
> I am the captain of my soul.
>
> W. E. Henley

It is not that sort of nonsense at all. A person who speaks like that in self-confidence is someone who always fails, and there are many ways in which we can do that. To become a cynic is failure. Just to resign yourself to life and its attendant circumstances is failure. And there are many like that. They do not solve the problem; they never get over the difficulties, nor do they ever know what it is to sing and to rejoice and to be filled with the spirit of exultation. No, there is no true victory there. At their best, self-confident people merely put up with things; they keep a stiff upper lip and brace their shoulders and go on with some philosophy of courage. But that is not what we have here. And others, of course, do not even do that. They just become complete failures, obviously defeated by the various temptations and trials of life.

But the thing about the psalmist is that he is filled with this spirit of assurance, of rejoicing and of praising, all of which is due to the fact that his confidence is not in himself. So the first thing we must always learn in this world, the first great characteristic of us as Christian people, is that we are no longer self-confident. We know the truth about ourselves. Like the Apostle Paul, we realise that 'we wrestle not against flesh and blood, but against principalities, against powers, against the rulers of the darkness of this world, against spiritual wickedness in high [or heavenly] places' (Eph 6:12). We know what we are up against and we realise our own utter weakness and helplessness: 'I had fainted unless I had believed to see the goodness of the Lord in the land of the living.'

That, then, is the first point, which is a negative but an all-important one. If you feel that you are competent to stand up to life, and that you can deal with all these things that are set against you, you are the merest tyro, an ignoramus; you do not really understand the problems and you do not understand yourself. No, this man's confidence is not based upon himself, and he makes it quite plain as to what the source of his confidence is: it is *'the Lord'*.

This, too, is always a distinguishing mark of the Christian. Our confidence is entirely and altogether in the Lord. The psalmist brings this out in a tremendous manner: 'The Lord is my light and my salvation'. He starts with the Lord. And how does he end? 'Wait, I say, on the Lord.' He begins with Him and he ends with Him. Altogether, in this psalm of fourteen verses, he mentions the name of the Lord thirteen times: six times in the first section, four times in the second section and three times in the third.

But not only that, he starts the first section with Him: 'The Lord is my light and my salvation', and ends it by saying, 'I will sing, yea, I will sing praises unto the Lord.' Then he starts the second section with 'Hear, O Lord, when I cry unto thee'. And on he goes: 'Thy face, Lord, will I seek'; 'the Lord will take me up'; 'the goodness of the Lord...', right down to his final exhortation to us, which he repeats: 'Wait, I say, on the Lord'.

Here is the whole secret: it is the Lord. It is not man himself, it is not the believer. It is his confidence in the Lord. On what does he base it? What is the Lord to him? Well, he gives us the answer: 'The Lord is my light'. And it does not need much imagination to know what he means by that. Light is the opposite to darkness, the opposite to despair. The gospel itself, in a sense, is introduced

147

to us in that way: 'The people which sat in darkness have seen a great light' (Mt 4:16).

What happens to us all as the result of these troubles and tribulations in life is that we are in darkness. We do not understand, so we say, 'Why should these things be happening? Why should I have to endure all this? I've tried to do this and that; I've tried to be godly and religious, but this is what is happening to me.' So we are in trouble and in darkness. Not only that, we do not see what we can do about it. We seek for solutions, and this is the whole story of civilisation. The world has been seeking for light, for answers to the problems. It is the whole meaning of philosophy and all the efforts of statesman and governments, trying to find some light to illumine the darkness, to find a way out and a way of deliverance. But there is none.

And so the whole world is in darkness and the people of today have given up—the characteristic of our age is cynicism. We see it in public entertainment: 'What's the use of anything; distrust everybody'; and people think it is funny and amusing. It is a terrible commentary on life, and it is tragic. Such people do not believe in anybody or anything any longer. That is darkness and that is humanity when left to itself. The problems are obviously so gigantic and immense and people cannot begin to understand them so they sit down, finally, in utter hopelessness and despair— 'There is nothing to be done', they say.

But, 'The Lord is my light'. Of course He is! It is the only light that is in the world today. Look at the light which these children of Israel had; they had more than anybody else. In spite of all their grumbling and all their disobedience, they knew certain things that nobody else did and that is why they stand out as the greatest people under the old dispensation. That is why their civilisation was a purer one and a better one, compared with the life of paganism as you can read about it in the history of the Greeks and the Romans and all the others. The Lord had given them light through the Law that He gave to Moses. Then you come to the New Testament, and suddenly everything changes and one appears who can say, 'I am the light of the world: he that followeth me shall not walk in darkness, but shall have the light of life' (Jn

8:12); 'I am the way, the truth, and the life: no man cometh unto the Father but by me' (Jn 14:6).

Light and understanding; the whole thing is explained to us, and those who believe this revelation given by the Lord are not surprised that the world is as it is. We do not believe in something foolish like evolution and hold that the world is getting better and better; because we can see it, at the moment, getting worse and worse. We observe the futility and everything else, but we understand; we know that it is all due to man's rebellion against God. We do not expect any different. We have light on the situation, we are no longer defeated because we see another way; another kind of life; the way out. 'The Lord is my light'. It does not matter what problem confronts the Christian. We can always find light on it in the Bible, it never fails: 'The Lord is my light and'—therefore— 'my salvation', my deliverer. He is the one who guarantees my welfare, the one who shows me the way to escape. Again, to quote Paul, we can be made 'more than conquerors' with the reserves, the power and all the things that He gives.

So the Lord is light and He is salvation. He is our deliverance, He is an emancipator, and what He does is to deliver us from the thraldom of this world. We are translated from the kingdom of darkness into the kingdom of God's dear Son. We belong to a different realm; though we are still in this world, our citizenship is in heaven. And this is the thing that means salvation; there is a translation, a deliverance, a movement, and we are taken out of it all. It is not that we do not have to suffer, but we are taken out of it in understanding and in spirit, and are put into this position of peace and rest and safety.

Then, thirdly, the psalmist goes on to say that 'the Lord is the strength of my life'. This, again, is a theme that runs right through the Bible. He is referring here, of course, to the power of the Lord. He sees the enemies; he is no fool. He can assess their strength. He knows the number of their battalions and of their dispositions: 'though war should rise against me'. He is fully aware of all this and of his own weakness. But he has a power behind him, a reserve; he has one who understands and who is illimitable in all His resources and all His power. He rises and all his enemies are scattered. 'The Lord is the strength of my life, of whom shall I be afraid?' As the old hymn puts it:

> A Sovereign Protector I have,
> Unseen, yet forever at hand,
> Unchangeably faithful to save,
> Almighty, to rule and command.
> He smiles, and my comforts abound;
> His grace like the dew shall descend,
> And walls of salvation surround
> The soul, He delights to defend.
>
> Augustus Toplady (1740–1778)

Or, as Martin Luther put it:

> A safe stronghold our God is still,
> A trusty shield and weapon,
> He'll help us clear from all the ill,
> That hath us now o'er taken.
>
> Tr. Thomas Carlyle (1795–1881)

This, you see, is the source of the psalmist's confidence. He knows that this is true about God: 'God is light, and in Him is no darkness at all' (1 Jn 1:5). God is wisdom; God is knowledge; God is all these to perfection. And then, add to that His might and His power and the strength of His arm—the irresistible God!

But the psalmist also knows other things about God lest we be frightened by His glory and greatness. This man knows about God's concern for us. He says, in the eighth verse, 'When thou saidst, "Seek ye my face"; my heart said unto thee, "Thy face, Lord, will I seek." ' Though He is so great and high and though He does not need us, we are His people. He is concerned for us and He invites us to come to Him. When we are in trouble, He, in various ways, comes to us and says, 'Seek my face'—'turn to me— roll your burdens onto me.' God comes to us even when we are overwhelmed by troubles and we are beginning to turn to human expediency and we do not know what to do. When we are utterly bewildered and frustrated, suddenly something says within us, 'Why not turn to God?' It is God Himself who is doing it by the Spirit. He prompts us: 'Seek my face. You see, you've forgotten me.'

And this is the great word of the whole Bible: 'Come unto me, all ye that labour and are heavy-laden, and I will give you rest' (Mt 11:28). Or, as we find Peter putting it in 1 Peter 5:8–9, 'Your adversary, the devil, as a roaring lion, walketh about, seeking whom he may devour: Whom resist, steadfast in the faith.' How do you do this? 'Well, there is only one way to do it,' says Peter, in effect, 'Cast all your care upon Him' (v 7). Why should I do so? Because 'He careth for you'. He knows all about you; He is interested. 'The very hairs of your head are all numbered,' said Jesus Christ (Mt 10:30). Nothing can happen to you apart from Him.

Not only that, there is one seated at the right hand of the Father who has been in this world and knows all about it. He suffered all that we suffer; He suffered the contradiction of sinners against Himself; He resisted unto blood; He understands all about the travail and the agony and all the weakness of flesh. He knows it all because He came in the likeness of sinful flesh and so, with His great care and concern, God says, 'Seek ye my face.' He encourages us to come to Him. He is not only there and ready and willing and waiting to help us, He even has to prompt us to come to Him in prayer. The hymn writer, Toplady, knew it so well from experience. God is not merely the hearer of prayer, He is the inspirer of prayer also:

> Inspirer and Hearer of prayer,
> Thou Shepherd and Guardian of Thine,
> My all to Thy covenant care,
> I sleeping and waking resign.

This is the basis of the psalmist's confidence.

And then, in verse 10, he says, 'When my father and my mother forsake me, then the Lord will *take me up*.' This is a blessed phrase because we struggle, we stumble and we fall, do we not? There we are, lying on the ground, unable to pick ourselves up and nobody else can do so either. But this everlasting and eternal God is ever ready to take us up. He takes hold of us; gets us onto our feet and establishes our goings. He is always ready to stoop to our weakness, mighty as He is.

In the same verse, we find our final confidence: *His unchangeableness*. 'When my father and my mother forsake me, then the Lord will take me up.' Thank God for fathers and mothers, but they are fallible. They are only human; they are sinful; and they have often forsaken us. Indeed, there are many people who have been forsaken by their father and mother simply because they have become Christians. The love of a father and a mother is a wonderful thing, but one of the great tragedies of life is that there are points at which it fails. We are all changeable; we cannot be relied upon in an ultimate sense. There is only one of whom that is true, and that is God. As one of our hymns puts it:

> Can a woman's tender care
> Cease towards the child she bare?
> Yes, she may forgetful be,
> Yet will I remember Thee.

Then God speaks:

> Mine is an unchanging love,
> Higher than the heights above,
> Deeper than the depths beneath,
> Free and faithful, strong as death.
>
> William Cowper (1731–1800)

You see, even though it does not turn its back upon us, there is a point beyond which human love cannot go, even when it wants to. There are certain secret problems, there are agonies of the soul where a father and a mother cannot help. But God still can! And even in the agony of death, when all human aid has failed, God is still with us. There, then, is the basis and source of this psalmist's confidence. He knows that these things are true of God, and while these things are true he is afraid of nothing. He can challenge the whole universe. With such a God, it matters not what rises against him.

So, I ask a question again: do you face life like this? Are you 'more than conqueror'? If not, you will be anxious to ask the question, 'How can I get this confidence? How can I attain to the position of the psalmist? How can I not only get it, but maintain it and continue with it?' But he has anticipated you, and written his psalm in order to help you. And here are his answers.

The first great thing is: *believe in the Lord*. 'I had fainted unless I had believed' is always the beginning. You cannot have anything without belief. The author of the Epistle to the Hebrews says, 'He that cometh to God must believe that He is, and that He is a rewarder of them that diligently seek Him' (Heb 11:6). I have nothing to offer you if you do not believe in God. I leave you to the utter despair and horror, the final bankruptcy, of some of those clever people who vaunt their unbelief and their nothingness on the television. There is nothing, nothing at all, apart from belief in God. Accept the revelation, humble yourself, become a little child, and believe the truth.

But even that is not enough. There are people who believe the truth about God as it is revealed in the Bible and yet remain in trouble and defeated. Why? Because they have not gone on to do the other things that this man tells us. Belief is the starting point and only the starting point. You can be a Christian and yet be miserable and unhappy because you fail to go on to the second point which he emphasises in verse 4: 'One thing have I desired of the Lord, that will I seek after; that I may dwell in the house of the Lord, all the days of my life, to behold the beauty of the Lord, and to enquire in his temple.'

It is this 'one thing', this total concentration upon God. 'Isn't it enough?' you say. 'I've always believed in God.' People have often told me, 'I've always believed in God. I've always said my prayers.' And yet they are full of troubles and problems and defeat, because a mere belief in God is of no value. 'The devils also believe and tremble,' says James (Jas 2:19). But you must concentrate. God must become the supreme thing in your life. He must be the one object of your desire and of your ambition.

This, too, is found throughout the Scriptures. The Apostle Paul, at the height of his great experience, says that this is his desire, the one thing that he wants. 'That I may know him, and the power of his resurrection, and the fellowship of his sufferings' (Phil 3:10). 'This one thing I do, forgetting those things which are behind..., I press toward the mark' (Phil 3:13–14). It is the realisation that nothing really matters ultimately in life except my relationship to God: 'That I may dwell in the house of the Lord all the days of my life.'

This does not just mean a physical building. Nor does it mean just that you want to spend the whole of your time in a chapel or a church—that is only a part of it. What he really means is this: 'That I belong to the household of God; that I am ever in communion with God; in fellowship with God; in touch with Him'. In effect, the psalmist is saying, 'What I want above everything else in this world is always to be in that intimate relationship to God so that whatever happens, I am with Him and He is with me.' This is the one thing he wants. This is the first thing in his life and that is the secret of his whole position.

Then, what does he desire and what does he dwell on? And here again, I want you to notice the order of these things. This man's supreme desire is to worship God and to adore Him and so that is what he starts with: 'One thing have I desired of the Lord, that will I seek after; that I may dwell in the house of the Lord, all the days of my life.' What for? *'To behold the beauty of the Lord.'* He repeats it in the thirteenth verse: 'I had fainted unless I had believed to see the goodness of the Lord.'

Now a much better translation of the word rendered 'behold' in the Authorised Version would have been 'to gaze upon'; to meditate upon; to consider 'the beauty of the Lord'. It means to see the desirableness of God, to see His goodness, to consider and to meditate upon and to contemplate His excellences. This is what this man wants above everything else.

He does not start with answers to prayers and deliverance, or this and that particular blessing. Not at all! He wants to know God and to 'gaze upon' Him. This is adoration; this is worship! He is talking about the being of God, and about God's dealings with us.

His supreme ambition is to gaze upon the glory of the being of God. Let a poet express it for us:

> My God, how wonderful Thou art;
> Thy majesty, how bright,
> How beautiful Thy mercy-seat,
> In depths of burning light!
>
> How dread are Thine eternal years,
> O, Everlasting Lord,
> By prostrate spirits day and night
> Incessantly adored.
>
> How wonderful, how beautiful,
> The sight of Thee must be,
> Thine endless wisdom, boundless power,
> And awful purity!
>
> Frederick W. Faber (1814–63)

And the psalmist wanted to gaze upon that—the glory of God, the beauty of the Lord in His very being; the consideration of His attributes. Do you do this? Is this your supreme ambition? Is this your greatest desire? My dear friend, this is the whole secret of life! If you want to be 'more than conqueror', like this man, you must spend your time as he did. This must be your supreme desire.

Then he considers His dealings with us: 'the goodness of the Lord in the land of the living'. Let another poet express this:

> When all Thy mercies, O my God,
> My rising soul surveys,
> Transported with a view I'm lost,
> In wonder, love and praise!
>
> Joseph Addison (1672–1719)

Do you know anything about that? Does your soul rise as you contemplate these things? Do you know something of these transports of delight? But the question is: do you spend your time in 'gazing upon Him'? The psalmist starts with worship and adoration, and we also see this in the New Testament. 'We all with open face,' says Paul, 'beholding as in a glass, the glory of the Lord' (2 Cor 3:18). That is it; you 'set your affections on things above, not on things on the earth' (Col 3:2).

Having begun in this way, the psalmist comes on to praise: 'I will sing, yea, I will sing praises unto the Lord'. You see, this is the secret of this man. You say your prayers, do you not? And when you are in trouble, you go to God and ask for this blessing or that. But you do not get it, do you? And you say, 'What's the point of praying if my prayers are not answered?' Of course they are not— you do not know how to pray. You should never start with yourself and your petitions. You start with God and you gaze upon His glory; the glory of His person and of His works, and then you praise Him:

> Praise the Lord, His glories show,
> Saints within His courts below.
> Angels round His throne above,
> All that see and share His love.
>
> Praise the Lord, His mercies trace,
> Praise His providence and grace.
> All that He for men hath done,
> All He sends us through His Son.
>
> Henry Francis Lyte (1793–1847)

Do you praise God? When you are on your knees alone, do you just say your prayers mechanically? Or do you praise Him? Do you trace His providence and grace? Do you 'count your blessings and name them one by one'? And does your heart well up within you and outpour itself in praise and in thanksgiving? Because it is only after he has done all that, that the psalmist then takes his petitions to God: 'Hear, O Lord, when I cry with my voice: have mercy also upon me and answer me.... Hide not thy face far from me; put not thy servant away in anger: thou hast been my help; leave me not, neither forsake me, O God of my salvation.... Deliver me not over unto the will of mine enemies: for false witnesses are risen up against me, and such as breathe out cruelty' (vs 7,9,12).

Once more, have you understood this strategy of prayer? This is the way to pray. The Apostle Paul has said it all, as we have seen, in Philippians 4:6—'Be careful for nothing but in every thing'—or in all circumstances—'by prayer and supplication with thanksgiving let your requests be made known unto God.' There it is: you start with adoration, wonder and amazement. You gaze upon Him and all His glorious attributes: what He has been, what He has done for us and all the wonders of His work. You trace them out, you praise Him and then, knowing Him, you bring your petitions to Him whatever they may be.

Then, the psalmist says, having done all that, wait for the answer. Everything does not finish the moment you have uttered your petition. '*Wait* on the Lord.' He has heard you; He will do it and He will do it in His own way.

Then, finally, he comes to his inevitable conclusion. He says, 'You know, if I hadn't "believed to see the goodness of the Lord in the land of the living;" if I didn't know that God is ready and waiting to bless His people in this world as well as in that which is to come, "I would have fainted".'

So, he says to himself, 'Wait on the Lord: be of good courage and He shall strengthen thine heart: wait, I say, on the Lord.' Start like that and keep on like that. Make it the central thing of your life to gaze upon God, to arrive at a knowledge of Him that will be intimate and personal, a communion with Him that will ravish your heart and cause your soul to rise up with Him. 'Seek His face'—go on seeking it. 'Wait upon Him'—let us praise Him and put ourselves entirely and completely in His hands.

And if you do so, you will find that He will be your light; your salvation; your strength and power; your never-failing refuge:

> No earthly father loves like Thee,
> Nor mother, e'er so mild,
> Bears and forebears, as Thou hast done,
> With me, Thy sinful child.

> Father of Jesus, love's reward,
> What rapture will it be
> Prostrate before Thy throne to lie,
> And gaze and gaze on Thee.
>
> Frederick William Faber (1814–1863)

How wonderful—the beatific vision—the end at which all the true people of God who wait upon Him shall ultimately arrive!